Alexander Solzhenitsyn

STEVEN ALLABACK

Alexander Solzhenitsyn

Taplinger Publishing Company

New York

This edition first published in the United States in 1978 by
TAPLINGER PUBLISHING CO., INC.
New York, New York

Copyright © 1978 by Steven Allaback
All rights reserved. Printed in the U.S.A.

Published by arrangement with Warner Paperback Library,
a division of Warner Books, Inc.
75 Rockefeller Plaza, New York, N.Y. 10019

Library of Congress Cataloging in Publication Data

Allaback, Steven.
  Alexander Solzhenitsyn.

  Bibliography: p.
  1. Solzhenitsyn, Aleksandr Isaevich, 1918—
—Criticism and interpretation.   I. Title.
PG3488.04Z554   891.7′3′44   77-92765
ISBN 0-8008-0167-9

For Mark, Sarah, and Kate

CONTENTS

FOREWORD

Alexander Solzhenitsyn, a Writer for Our Time

Considering that his career as a published author began only about fifteen years ago, a great deal has been written about Alexander Solzhenitsyn. However, despite some excellent critical pieces (most of which are cited by Steven Allaback in this book), the bulk of the material on Solzhenitsyn has dealt less with the writer than with the man—his origins, his early life, his military service, his almost miraculous survival of the prison camps and of cancer, his life in exile, his early literary successes, his turbulent role as a dissenter, his literary excommunication, his Nobel Prize, his persecution and subsequent banishment from the Soviet Union, and his controversial career as an anti-Soviet spokesman and Christian apologist.

This emphasis on Solzhenitsyn the man is hardly surprising. With the possible exception of André Malraux, surely no twentieth-century writer has had a life more full of drama and adventure than Solzhenitsyn. Indeed, if he were a character in a novel, he'd strain credulity; he is a prime example of truth stranger than fiction. Few men of *any* century have experienced, suffered, endured—survived—more than he. Yet we do this Nobel Prize winner an injustice in stressing his life at the expense of his books. It is, after all, his literary works on which Solzhenitsyn's ultimate reputation will rest.

As Steven Allaback shows, Solzhenitsyn brings the very highest sense of literary mission to his writing. He not only takes his work seriously, he takes his audience seriously as well, assuming that he writes for readers earnestly concerned with the themes he explores in his novels. As Professor Allaback says, "Solzhenitsyn believes that literature is where you put serious matters. . . ."

Discussing *One Day in the Life of Ivan Denisovich*, Allaback notes Solzhenitsyn's "insistent, unremitting focus" on the details of Ivan Denisovich Shukov's existence: on boots, on cigarettes, on gruel, on warmth. The quoted phrase could also be used to describe what I think is the major virtue of Allaback's *Alexander Solzhenitsyn*. Throughout his study he focuses sharply on Solzhenitsyn's creation of a fictive "living world" (to borrow a term from Gleb Nerzhin in *The First Circle*), and he shows how deeply Solzhenitsyn's novels touch "the daily non-literary lives of most of us." The great power of Solzhenitsyn—of any major novelist—comes from his ability to create what Allaback calls "life in print." With both involvement and detachment, with passion and critical judgment, Allaback helps to bring out this created life in print for us.

Alexander Solzhenitsyn is very much a book for American readers. In addition to the other merits of his study, Allaback shows us how relevant—how very *necessary*—Solzhenitsyn is to us in the United States. "I am the man, I suffer'd, I was there," says our great American epic poet, Walt Whitman. Solzhenitsyn would have as much right to appropriate those words as any man who has ever lived. In *Song of Myself* Whitman also says, "I understand the large hearts of heroes." So, too, Solzhenitsyn. His heroes—men like Ivan Denisovich Shukhov, Gleb Nerzhin, Oleg Kostoglotov, Colonel Vorotyntsev—all have large hearts. But, and this is one of the most important things about Solzhenitsyn's work, they are not larger-than-life figures: not superheroes, but human beings. They are men who have been tested by suffering and temptation and have come through with their humanity intact. With their humanity enhanced.

As Allaback notes, Solzhenitsyn is stubbornly "old-fashioned" in his refusal to regard good and evil as relative or quaintly outdated terms. But Solzhenitsyn's characters are never mere ciphers in abstract morality dramas; instead, they are rounded creations struggling to achieve or retain their humanity. In observing their struggles (and noticing their false steps and slips), we can learn much about our own human capacities. Among other things, we can learn, as another American poet, Robinson Jeffers, expresses it, that "corruption/ Never has been compulsory."

Here we are more than halfway through the 1970s, three-quarters of the way through our splendid and appalling twentieth century—creeping up fast on 1984. Obviously, it would be important to have a writer like Solzhenitsyn around at any time. (When has the human race not had need of an author who conveys "the plain unvarnished truth" in his works?) Obviously, we've never had more need for such a "courage teacher" (Allen Ginsberg's term for Whitman). In his novels and in the Gulag Archipelago volumes, Solzhenitsyn teaches us much about the necessary conduct of life if one is to become (or remain) fully human; thereby, he teaches us much about the meaning of life. Which, I suppose, is more than anything else what great literature is about.

Steven Allaback's *Alexander Solzhenitsyn* helps us to

11

get at this necessary and imperishable element in Solzhenitsyn's work. It helps us to *feel* the absolute importance
of "the character of individual men."

Terence Malley
Long Island University
Brooklyn Center

PREFACE

In the summer of 1975 Alexander Solzhenitsyn made a brief but highly publicized visit to the United States. For a time it seemed that not only the President and the Secretary of State but every columnist and editorial writer in the country had an opinion about him. We were interested in this man and even eager to regard him as a hero. Nevertheless, there were hollow notes in the acclaim, as if many of those giving it were caught off guard and had not themselves actually read the fiction on which his reputation ultimately will rest but instead based their response on his public statements and lectures, on second-hand information, perhaps on a portion of the first volume of *The Gulag Archipelago*.[1] Except for an infrequent reference to Ivan Denisovich, the characters in Solzhenitsyn's fiction went unnoticed. And why not? Most of the commentators were understandably more fascinated by the man and his politics than by the writer and his fiction.

Solzhenitsyn had won the Nobel Prize, he had been expelled from the Soviet Union, he was the subject of an international controversy, he carried himself with the impressive gravity of a survivor, and although he said some ridiculous things during his visit, he himself never became ridiculous. As a public figure, he was, and is, undeniably interesting.

I have no way of proving this, but I suspect his American visit (along with his earlier expulsion from his own country) made an increasing number of people turn to the fiction-behind-the man. I know many of my neighbors did. And many academic readers of my acquaintance who had previously dismissed him as merely a political protest writer, a reactionary, a Christian mystic, a neo-Slavophile, a heavy-handed stylist, a didactic bore, began to read him for the first time or took him more seriously than ever before. At any rate, a lot of people *are* reading Solzhenitsyn right now. Undoubtedly, some continue to find him heavy going, but this book is addressed to those who, like myself, find him an important novelist who offers unexpected treasure to American readers. The experts in Russian language and literature have been telling us that all along, but often the very form of their telling has made Solzhenitsyn seem remote and inaccessible.

This book focuses upon selected characters and scenes in Solzhenitsyn's four novels. The "Solzhenitsyn" to whom I will be confidently and constantly referring is an entity derived from the fiction and is not necessarily the flesh-and-blood man, unless otherwise noted. Although occasionally I do use biographical information and passages from the *Gulag* volumes and other nonfictional writings, I do so to buttress my discussion of the fiction. My ideal reader would be a person who had read all or most of Solzhenitsyn and who wished to compare his or her impressions and opinions with those of someone else. I discuss those features of each novel which seem to me interesting and important and which also help to illuminate Solzhenitsyn's work as a whole. I begin each chapter with a few general remarks on the book in question, followed by a summary of the action, and then I give a rather detailed commentary, in which I explain, judge, opine, speculate, and observe. The chapter on *Ivan Denisovich* is disproportionately long because in that work Solzhenitsyn, uncharacteristically, provides comparatively little of his own commentary, hence leaving more to the reader—that is, to me. I usually move from a specific character to a general proposition of one kind or another and back again to a specific character, a way of suggesting what I believe to be true, that the life of characters is more important in fiction than the promulgation of ideas —though one can hardly ignore ideas, especially in the work of Solzhenitsyn. I am not, however, pursuing a single thesis so much as taking the attitude that in a book like this, a kind of introduction to Solzhenitsyn, I have the luxury of hinting at more theses than I actually pursue. I am searching primarily for evidence of life in print and am assuming that to explain what I mean by "life" would be tedious and unnecessary. Marvin Mudrick says it better than I can:

> Life isn't always easy to recognize in print, it may be diffused over many pages of incident and contingency, it may go by in a phrase or a barely perceptible turn of events while the reader's attention wanders, it may too quickly get lost or mangled in the machinery; but the reader of fiction has no alternative to looking for it, since everything else is already laid out in Northrop Frye's elegant Linnaean categories, or Wayne Booth's conventional morality disguised as an inventory of handy devices, or Ian Watt's sociology, or Albert Guerard's Jungian recipes, or R. S. Crane's infatuation with thoroughly lubricated plots, or F. R. Leavis's rack-and-thumbscrew culture-obsession.[2]

And so on.

Even though I quote extensively, because I do not read Russian myself I avoid commenting upon the nuances of the verbal surface of Solzhenitsyn's prose. Milton Ehre has said that in the original Russian Solzhenitsyn's language is "innovative and daring"; Vera Carpovich has pointed out the "lexical peculiarities" of his vocabulary; Nikita Struve believes that he has returned "vitality, verve, and color to the Russian language,"[3] and many experts have noted how much of Solzhenitsyn's richness is lost in translation. Nevertheless, my entire commentary is based on the most accessible paperback volumes of translated Solzhenitsyn, not on the original Russian. Alexis Klimoff, who has written authoritatively on the subject, poses the question of whether it is even worth the effort to read Solzhenitsyn in English. His answer:

> . . . yes, for in spite of the countless infelicities, mistakes, revisions, and "corrections," the prose of this verbal master still produces a powerful and sometimes overwhelming effect. This is not because a poor translation does little damage—the opposite is surely true—but because Solzhenitsyn's work is so rich in thought, imagery, and texture, that even an imperfect or partial rendering retains abundant literary worth.[4]

I am indebted to the work of others. The most readily available sourcebook, upon which I depend heavily, is the invaluable *Aleksandr Solzhenitsyn: Critical Essays and Documentary Material*, edited by John B. Dunlop, Richard Haugh, and Alexis Klimoff. In addition to the work of these three, I profited greatly from the writings of Michael Scammell, Michael Glenny, Helen Muchnic, Victor Erlich, Mary McCarthy, Philip Rahv, Irving Howe, Alexander Schmemann, Kathryn B. Feuer, Georg Lukacs, and many others, most of whom are mentioned in the notes. Despite its imperfections and lack of documentation, the best biography to date is David Burg and George Feifer's *Solzhenitsyn* (New York: Stein and Day, 1972). Rosette Lamont, Kathryn B. Feuer, Mary McCarthy, Helene Zamoyska, and Gleb Struve (all of whom have portions of their work in *Dunlop*) are especially effective in placing Solzhenitsyn in the context of Russian literature and culture, a task which I do not assume in this book. I am also grateful for the innumerable specific suggestions offered by Larry Adams of Baruch College, CUNY, and by my editor, Terence Malley of Long Island University, and for the advice and encouragement of my colleagues at Santa Barbara, Stephen Miko, Marvin Mudrick, John and Muriel Ridland, and Lawrence Willson. Ms. Melanie Ito typed the manuscript and offered further suggestions along the way.

CHAPTER ONE

One Day in the Life of
Ivan Denisovich

Of all Solzhenitsyn's novels, *One Day in the Life of Ivan Denisovich* is the easiest to follow: it is short; the prose style, like the main character, seems simple and straightforward; there are no complicated maneuvers in the plot; the reader never finds himself lost. Unlike *The First Circle* and *August 1914*, *Ivan Denisovich* does not demand that we keep consulting a list of characters or a battlefield map at the beginning. After the first few pages you know you can finish it in an afternoon.

But for a novel set in a Soviet prison camp populated by men who live exceedingly close to the bone and which has the power to force us to reassess our own values as well as shudder at the horror of the lives before us, *Ivan Denisovich* is curiously difficult to picture and, at times, even to remember. It is a novel of brief encounters and vivid moments, not scenes. At the end we know Shukhov well enough, and we probably have an impression of the

18

novel's tone (determinedly cheerful) and color (gray) and temperature (frozen). But those extended descriptions of setting and topography, of the personal characteristics, histories, and idioms of the characters, of the entire look and feel of the situation which we so often have in Solzhenitsyn's other novels are lacking here—though that is not necessarily a loss to grieve over, as we shall see later on. What scene-painting exists in *Ivan Denisovich* is done lightly; a biography of a minor character is given in only one or two lines; there is a deliberate economy of language, even a deliberate vagueness, as if the author does *not* wish to particularize the prison camp— for fear of making it seem merely unique, the only one of its kind.

Although nothing much "happens" in this novel about one unusually good day in the life of an ordinary prisoner, it is nevertheless full of movement, perhaps too much movement for such a short novel, with Shukhov at times dashing about almost frenetically. There are flashbacks; switches in point of view; and interruptions, including new narrative voices now and then as well as new minor characters. None of these devices creates as much confusion as, for instance, some readers claim to find in the troop movements in *August 1914*, but their use does mean that *Ivan Denisovich* rarely holds steady. It is difficult for a reader to live with a situation long enough to appropriate it. It is not that we fail to remember *moments* —Shukhov savoring his meals, for example—but I suspect that for most readers the setting for these moments (except the very broadest context, the prison camp itself) remains cloudy in memory.

At five o'clock in the morning reveille at the prison camp is sounded by a hammer banging against steel. Shukhov awakens, but he feels ill, and so instead of jumping from bed as he usually does to take advantage of the hour-and-a-half before roll call, he stays there and thinks about his situation, which includes the possibility of getting on the sick list for today. Other prisoners rise, and the barracks begin to come to life. Suddenly a Tartar warder enters, notices Shukhov still in bed, and takes him away—not to the commandant's office for punishment but to the warders' room to mop the floor. He mops it, but not well. The warders seem to him "dopes" rather than "human beings."[1] From the warders' room he goes to the mess hall for his breakfast: cabbage gruel with fish skeletons and mush made from magara. After breakfast he makes his way to the hospital, where a young medic and would-be poet named Vdovushkin takes his temperature (not quite 99°) and recommends that he go on to work rather than see a doctor (if Shukhov is found to be malingering, he lands in the cooler). Shukhov returns to his barracks where he receives his bread ration ("about half an ounce short"); he tucks half of it in a hole in his mattress and the other half in a pocket which he has sewn in his jacket. Then the gang boss yells, "Outside!" and the prisoners file out and line up for roll call. It is still dark.

After roll call Shukhov notices that his number is beginning to fade, and so he has it repainted by one of the artists. He then returns to his gang where Caesar, a former movie cameraman and a person who receives two packages a month from home, is smoking a cigarette. The scavenger Fetyukov watches with "burning eyes" (33), but when Caesar finishes the cigarette, he gives the butt to Shukhov, not Fetyukov. It is his first victory of the day. As the prisoners prepare to leave the camp compound for the construction site, they are frisked by the warders. Wolf-like Lieutenant Volkovy, the disciplinary officer, looks on. The prisoners go through the gates and are turned over to guards with tommy guns and dogs. They line up by fives and are marched toward the construction site. The prisoners pass by the living quarters and recreation facilities of the "free" workers and then emerge "into the steppe with the wind right in their faces. . . ." It is sunrise. "Bare white snow lay as far as the eye could see and there wasn't a tree in sight" (44).

They finally reach the construction site. Shukhov has

an aching pain in his back, and his hands are frozen. As the prisoners wait for the guards to take their places in the watchtowers overlooking the site, Shukhov stands "with his back to the wind" (49), but the moment the guards are set and the prisoners allowed inside, Shukhov and his gang (Gang 104) move quickly to the repair shop where they are able to find a "warm spot" (52) before beginning the day. Meanwhile, the boss of Gang 104, Tyurin (a camp veteran whom Shukhov admires), has gone to the work office to determine the day's assignment. When he returns, the men learn that their project is the unfinished power plant which they had stopped work on in the autumn (it is now January). Tyurin tells Shukhov and Kilgas (a Latvian bricklayer) that they will be laying bricks after the meal break, but first they are to find a way to cover the windows in the generator room (to keep out the cold), where the mortar will be mixed. Shukhov runs off to find his good-fitting trowel which he had secreted away the previous day, and then he and Kilgas (also admired by Shukhov because "he knew his way around" [61]) set out together to steal a roll of roofing-felt from another area of the site. When they return to the power plant Shukhov is asked to fix the flue on the stove; he does this while at the same time helping to supervise the installation of the roofing-felt window covers. The gang spend the morning preparing for the bricklaying.

At the noon meal break Shukhov has a run of good luck. First he discovers that today's mush is "the best kind, made of oats" (84), and then through a clever bit of maneuvering he is able to get two extra bowls for his gang, one of which he eventually eats himself. The other bowl is given to the Captain, a former naval officer and a new prisoner who has yet to learn his way around the camps. Near the end of the meal break, after carrying a bowl of mush to Caesar (who has bribed his way into a soft job in the office), Shukhov finds a chunk of metal sticking out of the snow. "He could think of no particular use for it, but you never knew when something might come in handy" (95). When he gets back to the power plant where the men are telling stories and warming themselves around the stove before going back to work, he acquires a cigarette. As he smokes it he wonders who among his gang should receive the butt.

In the afternoon Shukhov and Kilgas begin to lay bricks for a wall on the second story. Shukhov works hard and well, losing track of time, shouting for more mortar, getting to the point where he doesn't "feel the cold anymore" (111). He himself becomes "a sort of gang boss for a time" (111). Work is interrupted when the building foreman (Der, a former Moscow bureaucrat) enters the power plant and complains about the roofing-felt over the windows, but he is driven off by the tough gang boss, Tyurin. The wall continues to grow higher. The men are caught up in the job, and when the whistle sounds they continue to work, Shukhov lingering over the wall even after everyone else at the construction site is lining up for the march back to camp. In fact, he keeps the other prisoners waiting so long that they start screaming at him. It is now dark and the moon is rising. They line up by fives again and are counted, but this time one man seems to be missing; cold, hungry, upset at the loss of a precious end-of-the-day half hour, the prisoners yell angry insults at the missing man even after the guards find him on the scaffolding where he had gotten warm and fallen asleep.

Finally, the column is ready. But having already lost so much time and now reconciled to being the last group back to camp, the prisoners march slowly, "their eyes on the ground like they were on their way to a funeral" (141). Then all at once the men in front of Shukhov begin to increase the pace; another column (from the tool works) has been spotted across the plain; theirs is not the last one out after all. The two columns race each other toward camp. Time will be saved if they beat the others, and they do. Everyone in Shukhov's column "was on top of the world" (145). At the gates of the camp the prisoners drop the bundles of scrap firewood they had collected at the construction site, and then they line up to be frisked. Shukhov suddenly discovers the chunk of steel in his pocket; he transfers it to one of his mittens and is able to smuggle it past one of the guards. Once inside, he decides to stand in line at the package room, not because he expects a package but because Caesar does, and Shukhov sees the chance to receive a little something for holding Caesar's place in line.

As soon as Caesar comes to take his place (telling Shukhov to take his supper), Shukhov walks across the compound to the steps of the mess hall. Here various gangs are competing for entrance, shoving each other around and pushing against Clubfoot, the mess hall orderly, who lets the gangs in one at a time when he is ready. The moment Shukhov is inside the hall he spots an empty tray, pushes a smaller man aside to get it, and takes it over to Pavlo, the assistant gang boss, who is standing near the kitchen and needs the tray to help the gang get their supper bowls to the table quickly and easily. Shukhov is able to carry one of his gang's trays himself, placing it on the table in such a way that "the two best bowls would be on the side he was going to sit at" (168). He begins to eat his unusually large supper: two bowls of gruel (his and Caesar's) and two rations of bread (he receives ten ounces today instead of six because of his extraordinary output on the brick wall). He decides to save the bread for later. As he very carefully and slowly eats, he thinks that this is "what a prisoner lived for, this one little moment" (169).

After supper, he goes to a different part of the compound to dicker with the Latvian for some tobacco. He returns to his own barracks where he pays back a pinch of tobacco to the Estonian, who had loaned him a pinch at noon, and then he climbs into his bunk and nibbles at his bread and overhears several conversations. Next to him Caesar is opening his package from home; Shukhov loans Caesar his (illegal) penknife to help unwrap the treasures, but pretends to be uninterested in them. As the evening comes to an end the trustee in charge of their barracks calls them outside for the night check, but

23

Caesar is caught unprepared, his treasures vulnerable to anyone who might happen along. Shukhov feels sorry for him ("he didn't know a thing about life" [188]) and quickly conceives a plan to help him protect his goods during the check. Shukhov has had such a good day that he doesn't even mind going out in the cold. "It wasn't so bad standing here when you'd eaten a little bread and had a cigarette in your mouth" (190–1).

After the check, he returns to his bunk where he discusses prayer, God, and Christianity with his neighbor, Alyoshka-the-Baptist. Just when the prisoners are about to fall asleep, a warder enters the barracks to announce a second check. At this point Shukhov gives him "two cookies, two lumps of sugar, and a slice of sausage" (200), and he in turn offers to hide Caesar's bag under his pillow. They go outside again. They return. Shukhov gives one of the cookies to Alyoshka and then begins to chew the piece of sausage, savoring its juices, and thinks about all the good luck he has had today. He falls asleep, "almost happy."

I would like to begin this commentary by dismissing an approach to *Ivan Denisovich* which students of modernism, politics, catastrophe, and irony may be tempted to follow. It might be put something like this:

Although the novel begins with Ivan Denisovich Shukhov ill and ends with him "almost happy," his illness having vanished during what appears to be a very good day, his morning illness is actually psychological and symbolic of his condition as a prisoner-citizen in an unspeakably ghastly Soviet institution. His restoration to health and happiness by evening is merely a rhetorical device and the greatest irony in a novel full of ironies. Because he is lucky enough to lose himself in a job of satisfying work for a change, because he accidentally discovers a potentially valuable chunk of steel in the snow, because he happens to receive far more to eat this day than his usual pitiful ration, and because he himself is neither sensitive nor intelligent enough to see the larger picture of his condition (as we do), he manages to convince himself that there is hope, that his morning "illness" has been cured. The reader is supposed to know better: Shukhov's evening optimism is a delusion; he fools himself, his ignorance breeds bliss. Although Shukhov has made the adjustments necessary to survive with some contentment in the prison camp, the reader has all along been in the position of seeing through this cheerful ignorant peasant (a man who does not even know what happens to the moon in daytime) and checking off horror after horror, making a list of indictments against the Soviet system which Shukhov himself would never make. The purpose of the book is not so much to portray the life of Ivan Denisovich as it is to leave the reader seething with outrage at the murderous injustice of modern Russian life and to make a statement about man's inhumanity to man in the twentieth century. The last thing in the world the novel is really about is one day in the life of one prisoner; the title has a special irony of its own.

This approach is not all wrong. We are supposed to see more than Shukhov does. And we would be living in a literary fog if we were to ignore the historical fact that, as Terrance Des Pres puts it, Shukhov's story was "the fate of thousands of Russian POWs—the victims of war and the criminal unpreparedness of Russian defenses, of Stalin in particular, the system in general."[2] But the details of Ivan Denisovich's hour-by-hour life matter more than any indictment of the Soviet system which the book provides. Such indictments are commonplace, and some of the best are from Solzhenitsyn's own pen. If we wish to feel pure outrage, *The Gulag Archipelago*, one of the most eloquently angry books ever written, provides us with hundreds of reasons. But *Ivan Denisovich* is about one man, not an entire system. Hence while any responsible reader will pause to ponder the larger political and social and economic forces at work on that one man, he may miss, if he keeps watch only for resounding indictments, the fact that Shukhov, perhaps more than any

25

other character in Solzhenitsyn, is a prime example of life in print.

Shukhov is kept alive partly because Solzhenitsyn conceives him as proceeding step by step, hour by hour, as men alive do. His reactions to the events of his day are interesting and instructive because they are a continuing comment on some rock-hard facts of individual men's lives everywhere, even (especially) for those of us living in comparative luxury, in the West, a world away from the prison camp. We never forget where Shukhov is as we read *Ivan Denisovich*—it is the overwhelming fact of the book—but after only a few pages we should see that the tone and manner of the prose is not soliciting the reader's sympathy so much as his attention, as all deliberately understated prose styles do. The man before us is being squeezed under the excruciating pressure of prison; his life has been stripped to its bare essentials; almost everything has been taken from him—almost everything, but not quite everything. What does he have left? What resources and personal values can he call upon to get through another day with his spirit intact? How does he manage to remain human under that pressure? Solzhenitsyn, through a tone stripped of stridency, often as matter-of-fact as Hemingway's, is suggesting that we watch Shukhov carefully for the answers.[3] The simple, uneducated peasant (one of a gallery of peasants in Solzhenitsyn, usually followers of an older and truer way of life and often, though not in this case, exceedingly didactic) knows some things we ought to know—or perhaps already know but have forgotten.

But for a moment at the beginning of the novel it is not clear that Shukhov *is* alive or capable of showing us much of anything. He seems dreary and lethargic:

> In his sleep he'd felt very sick and then again a little better. All the time he dreaded the morning.
> But the morning came, as it always did (3).

And then a few lines later: "Shukhov stayed in bed." It is

26

enough to make us wonder if we haven't been here before, but we soon learn that Shukhov really is sick and his back aches (no literary illness, probably a mild case of the flu). Right here, when we first meet him, he is at his lowest point; as soon as he begins to make contact with people, his lethargy will vanish and his attitude will change for the better. Perhaps Solzhenitsyn does intend to hint that even on a day which turns out to be unusually good for Shukhov there are at its beginning faint shadows of despair and hopelessness; one could hardly expect the prisoners to hop out of bed and start singing for joy. Shukhov *would* like to spend the day in bed—what a luxury it would be—and he even tries to arrange it later on.

But the real Shukhov is no slacker, and he is about as far from being someone in search of himself or of meaning in life as it is possible to be. There is no identity crisis here, no alienation. He knows who he is and where he is, and although this particular morning he is for a time preoccupied with his illness, his mind nevertheless registers his position exactly: "He was lying on the top bunk, with his blanket and overcoat over his head and both his feet tucked in the sleeve of his jacket" (3). He can interpret every sound he hears, he knows the implications of every move around him, and he has already run through the list of ways he could "scrounge a little something on the side" if he were feeling better. The fourth alternative on this list is to

go to the mess hall to pick up bowls from the tables and take piles of them to the dishwashers. That was another way of getting food, but there were always too many other people with the same idea. And the worst thing was that if there was something left in a bowl you started to lick it. You couldn't help it. And Shukhov could still hear the words of his first gang boss, Kuzyomin—an old camp hand who'd already been inside for twelve years in 1943. Once, by a fire in a forest

27

clearing, he'd said to a new batch of men just brought in from the front:

"It's the law of the jungle here, fellows. But even here you can live. The first to go is the guy who licks out bowls, puts his faith in the infirmary, or squeals to the screws."

He was dead right about this—though it didn't always work out that way with the fellows who squealed to the screws. They knew how to look after themselves. They got away with it and it was the other guys who suffered (2).

Shukhov knows "what is what in the camps" (1), and he has adjusted himself to the facts of life without being obliterated by that adjustment—not yet, anyway, although he cannot afford to be smug. He wishes to avoid the mess hall job because he knows that he too could become a bowl-licker and destroy the tiny measure of dignity he has left, which he preserves as carefully as fine crystal glass. He knows that there is a point where the needs of the body overwhelm the needs of the spirit, and he wishes to keep clear of that point; once there, the body wins, the spirit loses. It is no contest. (This particular conflict, one of Solzhenitsyn's favorites, takes other forms in other works.)

The passage above with its informative and characteristic digression, itself a way of presenting the energy of Shukhov's mind, suggests that Shukhov is an alert student of the culture and practices of prison life—that is, he does more than face facts, which is hard enough and certainly important. But he wishes to do more than survive minimally; he tries to gain an edge when he can, and he is intelligent enough to respect practical wisdom wherever he finds it. He has learned from the past by listening to his elders—in this case, next to a fire in a forest clearing! He has also learned enough on his own to qualify their knowledge somewhat. He has been hardened by eight years in the camps, but he still knows more about people than most of his fellow gang members and he remains

28

sensitive (not hyper-sensitive) to human weakness and suffering. One senses that even in a society packed with official rules and regulations, unofficial cultural taboos (bowl-licking, squealing), and ironclad ethics ("It's the law of the jungle here . . ."), Shukhov has just enough room by an inch or two, just enough air of his own to breathe. He can hardly be a rugged individualist, but he is no automaton, either. He is fighting to remain more or less a man, and much of the novel is about the details of that fight.

After a few pages of *Ivan Denisovich,* however, some readers may think it a crime to find Shukhov's day rather inspiring, as I do. Any man who is *forced* to ask so little from life and then intimidated by his circumstances to be satisfied with so little (warm feet, an extra bowl of gruel) is surely pathetic. No man should have to live like this, even though many do. Simple Shukhov's moments of "contentment" are pure irony. The reader should be in the position of observing that this man is allowed virtually nothing from life, not in the position of analyzing how much he manages to squeeze from his deprived circumstances. It is wrong to find the novel the least bit hopeful. In point of fact, *all* Shukhov does is survive, and if at times (such as this one lucky day) he appears to have an edge on the other prisoners, it simply doesn't matter. It is not enough. He is still in prison, and he is likely to die there. His feeble attempts to do battle against his situation are perhaps understandable but are also absurd and pathetic. The possibilities of attainable happiness have been so reduced for Shukhov that we can only shake our heads in dismay. When, for example, the Tartar takes him to the warders' room to mop the floor instead of throwing him in the can and Shukhov is "real pleased" and thanks "the Tartar for letting him off" (10) and when a few minutes later his "pains seemed to have stopped" and he feels "warmer," the reader should see that a life is being wasted here. Nothing at all is being preserved. Shukhov should not have to be grateful to the warder, nor should getting warm in the warders' room be the first good moment of his day (which it is).

But the matter-of-fact tone suggests that both dismay and grand theorizing about the larger wrongs of Shukhov's situation are inappropriate and beside the point. It is as if those things have been done before the book began. Life has already been worse for Shukhov (scurvy, Ust-Izhma, 1943), and he actually regards himself as pretty well off in this camp, a rather endearing attitude; he is a veteran survivor and more. As we watch him plunge his hands into the "steaming bucket" of water and gain some warmth on this frozen morning, we are watching someone intimately acquainted with the necessities of life. Such men are often good instructors. They can remind us of what we need and what we don't—and that can be inspiring.

It is easy enough to agree that, yes, of course we all need instruction now and then in what Thoreau calls "the gross necessaries of life" so we can regain "perspective" or count our blessings or cease taking so much for granted; and, yes, it is good to be reminded that we cannot begin to pursue happiness or do our duty until the minimum requirements of food, fuel, clothing, and shelter are met. But it costs most people nothing to agree to these simple truths. The world is full of amateur Spartans, renunciators, fasters, Thoreaus. People can be exceedingly glib on this subject—and Solzhenitsyn seems to be trying hard to combat this glibness. In *Ivan Denisovich* there is an insistent, unremitting focus on not merely the necessities, but the tiniest fragments of necessities (fish-bones, scraps of firewood, patches of cloth), as if to suggest that books about life close-to-the-bone have been written before, but here we are going one step closer. It is always bracing to know that there are men in the world who can make do with very little, but the scale of the things which can satisfy Shukhov is extraordinarily small —and his (trained) capacity to relish his day's discoveries is extraordinarily large. Over and over Solzhenitsyn moves the reader directly behind Shukhov as he conducts his mundane affairs, as, for example, when he monitors the warmth of his hands or keeps his eye on the warm spots in camp and at the construction site. Just as we always know how much money people have in a Jane Austen novel, we always know where the stoves are in *Ivan Denisovich* and who is sitting near them. And when Shukhov expresses his pleasure at getting warm (or other achievements of this scale) we are meant to feel with him that at the moment nothing else matters, nothing. We are reminded that even away from the moment, wherever one may be on the planet, maintaining body heat and keeping the fires lit are ancient and fundamentally valuable human tasks. "Try not to forget that, reader," Solzhenitsyn seems to be saying again and again. "It will do you good." We do forget it, though; how can we help it?

Before Shukov begins to mop the warders' room he thinks about "the footwear situation":

There'd been times when they'd gone around all winter without any felt boots at all, times when they hadn't even seen ordinary boots but only shoes made of birch bark or shoes of the "Chelyabinsk Tractor Factory model" (that is, made of strips of tires that left the marks of the tread behind them). Now the boot situation had begun to look up. In October—this because he'd once managed to wangle himself a trip to the stores with the number-two man in his gang—Shukhov had gotten a pair of sturdy boots with good strong toes that were roomy enough inside for two thicknesses of warm footcloths. For a week he was on top of the world and went around knocking his new heels together with joy. Then felt boots were issued in December and life was great. You didn't want to die (12).

Shukhov has so little that he knows that exact value of everything he does have; he is a supreme appreciator of his wealth; his world is so barren of objects that he is

31

truly one of those people upon whom nothing is lost. He deserves to have more, but it is also exhilarating to watch him appreciate, just as it must be to watch a starving man eat.

Solzhenitsyn makes it perhaps too easy for us to applaud a character's talent for making the best of things. We should not be misled by our enthusiasm. In the above passage (and others like it later on), important discriminations are being made. There are lines drawn in *Ivan Denisovich* between footwear and, say, cigarette butts— the lines between necessity, near necessity, and luxury —and there are lines drawn between the kinds of footwear available: birchbark or tire shoes, felt boots, leather boots. When Shukhov finds himself the owner of a new pair of sturdy leather boots, the quality of his entire life changes; suddenly he experiences "joy," which seems an almost childishly excessive response to new boots. Is this because he is only a simple peasant? Isn't he too easily satisfied to be real? The answer is no. Solzhenitsyn insists on this. Good boots bring joy because now one's feet will be warm and comfortable; warm feet give one an edge in the battle for survival. With boots like these, in fact, one has *more* than he needs; he has an advantage. The line is clearly drawn. And when Shukhov is issued felt boots *in addition* to the leather boots, life becomes "great." Ironical? Somewhat, but Solzhenitsyn is an expert on this subject, and you keep hearing a voice behind the lines: "Reader, I know you are not a simple peasant like Shukhov, but you too would have felt the same way."

After acquiring boots, he "didn't want to die," thinks Shukhov. The luxury of two pairs does not put him so far out in the sunshine that he becomes silly or thinks he has a bright future, but the two pairs do give him more even than an advantage over others; they give a positive margin of strength. Take one pair away and he still has another. In a step-by-step existence, it is especially nice to be well shod, and he is, and he is proud of it. He has equipped himself for the life at hand, and he has trained himself to think of no other—perhaps that is true wisdom.

When he has to return the boots, nothing in eight years of camp life hurts him more. Could it be that even cheerful Shukhov is separated from despair by two pair of boots? If one's feet are warm, one is likely to have a better outlook on life; it's almost as simple as that. Those boots (and a few other items of similar scale) mean the difference between keeping a will to live and allowing oneself slowly to give up and die. In Solzhenitsyn's world, it is very easy to give up, though Shukhov himself is not a quitter. But when he thinks, "life was great. You didn't want to die," we see that even he has known blackness sometime in the past. He goes to great lengths "to wangle a trip to the stores" to get those boots and then treats them "with loving care" not only because he needs boots; he needs to keep his spirit alive, too, and those boots are a (temporary) victory. Shukhov is a fighter and a winner, but even he is always dangerously close to losing everything he has gained. His is a balancing act. When he has to return the sturdy pair of boots, he loses more than boots: He has retreated backwards, one step closer to a darker place where men want to die, not live. Although he never does fall into that dark place (if someone stole all his boots, he might), much of the tension and excitement in this relatively plotless novel come from our wondering if Shukhov *will* keep his balance. Will he be able to keep on the sunny side of the line? Will he "wangle" enough to maintain his sense of himself as an efficient and alert member of his community?

Not only does Shukhov need a few small victories now and then, but the manner in which he achieves these victories is an issue in *Ivan Denisovich*. Because he knows the ropes and himself so well, because he is so much more fortunate than countless others around him, he also has room enough to keep watch on his own dignity, itself a kind of luxury. One of Shukhov's most interesting small victories (it is called a "great thing") is when he is able to beat out Fetyukov for Caesar's cigarette butt without saying a word (32–34).

Shukhov's number (S-854) has just been repainted,

and he seems all set for the day. He spots Caesar smoking a cigarette and promptly takes a position next to him, looking past instead of at him. Then Fetyukov arrives and "stood right in front of Caesar and stared with burning eyes at his mouth." Shukhov wants the cigarette ("right now he thought he'd rather have this butt than his freedom"), but he won't "stoop as low as Fetyukov and look straight at the guy's mouth." Shukhov's refusal to stoop is important; he keeps only a blossom of dignity, but it is enough. His need for the cigarette is urgent, he is willing to go pretty far (he "turned halfway" toward Caesar), but he is unwilling to go as far as poor drooling, twitching Fetyukov who finally *asks* Caesar for a drag. In the outside world, the very thought of cadging a butt reveals a beaten man, but here, depending on your manner of receiving it, you can show yourself to be a competent man by accepting one.

But isn't Fetyukov so low in the hierarchy of prisoners that he makes anyone look better by comparison? Although Shukhov is more clever than Fetyukov and wiser about people, isn't he too only a leech and a scavenger? One could argue that instead of retaining a measure of "dignity" Shukhov simply knows how to keep from offending others. He is a successful bootlicker who keeps his poise, whereas Fetyukov doesn't know how to conceal his feelings and desires. A truly admirable man would not be trying for Caesar's cigarette butt in the first place. Caesar, after all, toys with *both* Fetyukov and Shukhov.

Shukhov is alive as a character partly because he can disappoint us, as in passages like this one (Caesar has just twisted the cigarette butt out of the holder):

> Shukhov jumped (even though he'd thought Caesar would give it to him of his own accord). He took it with one hand, quickly and thankfully, and put his other hand underneath to guard against dropping it. He wasn't hurt because Caesar was squeamish about letting him smoke it in the holder (some people have clean mouths, others have foul mouths), and it didn't hurt his hardened

34

fingers when the butt burned right down to them. The great thing was that he'd beaten that scavenger Fetyukov to it, and here he was now smoking away till it burned his lips (34).

If it happens that we have over-invested Shukhov with dignity or a heroic capacity to resist his situation, or if (as is more likely) we are prepared to love and sentimentalize him, this passage is embarrassing, especially that hasty little gesture with the hands. There are many such moments in *Ivan Denisovich*, moments in which Shukhov becomes eager and obsequious at apparently no cost to himself. Neither are his feelings hurt by Caesar's squeamishness nor are his ("hardened") fingers hurt by the burning cigarette, and in addition he is happy to have beaten poor Fetyukov. In terms of personal dignity, he concedes much here; in return, he gains a cheap sense of victory and a cigarette butt. We know, however, that he is *aware* of everything he does and that while there may be others in camp who would not be so quick to jump after the butt, Shukhov swallows his pride once the butt has been offered—but not before. The line is thin, but it separates the men from the scavengers. Solzhenitsyn has already made the sad point about human beings forced to grovel for butts; he adds these lines, I suspect, to show that our hero is a hero only by a hair, and to keep us from thinking too well of him. This is a realistic, truthtelling novel which would be ruined by characters with unmixed motives.

Getting tobacco and cigarettes in *Ivan Denisovich* is not quite the same as getting adequate footwear, but is almost as important: A cigarette means an interval of pure pleasure and satisfaction, a brief captured moment of enjoyment that, unlike eating, you don't absolutely need (although it comes close: "The smoke seemed to go all through his hungry body and into his feet and head" [34]). For men of Shukhov's means, a cigarette is handled as if it were precious metal and is a signal to the reader of how nothing is taken for granted by his class of prisoners.

However much mental anguish exists in most men's lives, there are nevertheless plenty of small, hour-by-hour physical satisfactions which can be taken for granted— but this is not the case for Shukhov. He has to work at and worry about insuring his tobacco supply; it is a big thing (on this day he is out of tobacco until the evening, when he goes to the Latvian in Barracks 7 and buys two rubles' worth with money he has earned by doing odd jobs for other prisoners). The urge for a cigarette is a tiny, two-bit, nagging urge which when satisfied in *Ivan Denisovich* reveals how few satisfactions there are in life for these men; at the same time it provides occasion for Solzhenitsyn to show us a man who fully appreciates what is available. At the noon meal break Shukhov manages to borrow some tobacco from Eino:

> Shukhov had some newspaper. He tore a piece off, rolled a cigarette, and lit it with a cinder that had fallen between the boss's feet. And then he dragged and dragged on it, over and over again! He had a giddy feeling all over his body, like it was going to his feet as well as his head (99).

Rarely has a cigarette been so enjoyed in literature.

Shukhov's manner of achieving this small victory is exemplary. In order to get that cigarette, he has had to assure Eino of his reliability ("You know I won't gyp you" [99]). Eino has to check with his close friend ("They always shared and shared alike and wouldn't use a single shred of tobacco without the other knowing" [99]); Eino then measures out enough for one cigarette. It is a precise and careful transaction which involves not only a valuable commodity but Shukhov's integrity—*and* the bond of friendship between Eino and his pal. Like a bullfight in Hemingway, there is a proper way to conduct this transaction; more than a single cigarette is at stake. Shukhov manages to keep his poise; Fetyukov loses his:

> The minute he started to smoke, he saw a pair of

36

green eyes flashing at him from the other end of the shed. It was Fetyukov. He might have taken pity on that scavenger, but he'd been cadging already today. Shukhov had seen him at it. Better leave the butt for Senka Klevshin. He couldn't hear the boss's story, poor devil, and was just sitting there in front of the stove with his head on one side (99–100).

Fetyukov ruins things. I said that smoking a cigarette is a captured moment of enjoyment, but it is truer to say that never in *Ivan Denisovich* does a man experience anything good which is unalloyed. Even at the end of the novel when the subject suddenly seems to be "happiness," Shukhov is merely "almost happy." Shukhov's carefully worked-for moment described in the two passages above is tainted by the inevitable presence of green-eyed Fetyukov. But, more importantly, Shukhov is also distracted here by an ethical question which seems to arise whenever he has more than he "needs." The small margin he so often gains on this day he can certainly appreciate, but he cannot revel in it. He deserves an interval of pure, unalloyed self-indulgence, but something in him won't allow it. (In fact, though no saint, he has a conscience.) Shukhov's acquisition of wealth (a whole cigarette, not just a butt) automatically triggers two questions: Should I share it? With whom? So despite the repeated statement in *Ivan Denisovich* that in prison it is dog-eat-dog and every-man-for-himself, only a heartless person can enjoy his hard-earned cigarette (or extra gruel, or cookies) without its becoming a moral and ethical issue. Shukhov pities Senka Klevshin because he is deaf, because he is not pushy like Fetyukov, and because he had been in Buchenwald. Fetyukov was only a factory manager; Senka's credentials are far more impressive, and Shukhov finds him worthy of the cigarette butt. In the space of only a few lines, what begins as a simple action—one man trying to enjoy a cigarette—becomes a moral issue. When Shukhov chooses Senka over Fetyukov as the rightful heir to the cigarette butt, he is making a judgment of the sort which occurs everywhere in Solzhenitsyn's work.

In one way or another Shukhov judges everyone he meets. We are also meant to judge everyone Shukhov meets, as well as Shukhov himself, and by the end of the novel, as in all Solzhenitsyn's works, we should be able to say exactly where every character fits on a carefully calibrated moral scale. Shukhov does not make a show of moral judgments, nor does he agonize over them, nor would he call himself a judge or a moralist or even a man on the lookout for kindness (though he is). In fact, that side of him which is capable of pushing "goners" out of the way or which claims that you "could cheat anyone you liked in the camp, but not Tyurin" (50) shows an unhealthy respect for expediency and a somewhat calloused sensibility—but that is only one side of him. We are intended to see more of his world and himself than he does. Shukhov is basically a good man (or at least a man with good in him), but the prison does not allow him to be as good as he could be. He talks tougher than he feels, which is often the way of men under pressure.

One of the things that makes Solzhenitsyn unusual among contemporary writers is his refusal to regard good and evil as outdated, either as words or concepts. Judging a particular action as right or wrong is not merely a matter of one's point of view; a reliable and absolute guide to morality exists. But in *Ivan Denisovich*, where does it come from? God? The Russian Church? An inner light? Peasant wisdom? Solzhenitsyn himself does not seem sure, not in *Ivan Denisovich*—and I say this even though today it is common knowledge that Solzhenitsyn is emphatically a Christian and even though his later work emphatically clarifies the sources of his moral position. Sources aside for the time being, the moral standard in this novel is as real as cigarettes and boots, though some characters cannot see it and would deny it if they could see it. As Shukhov proceeds step by step through the day, his mind alert and his eyes as sharp as an eagle's, he is not purposely conducting an inquiry into human behavior, yet he registers every nuance of kindness, every tiny sliver of hate and injustice.

He has, however, already spent eight years in prison, and for no good reason. Isn't he used to living in a fallen world by now? The larger wrong, the mammoth injustice, has *already* been committed; that he and millions like him are here in the first place suggests a moral disease in high places so infectious that one would not expect Shukhov to be surprised or alarmed to find it in low places too. And he isn't. Practically the first conversation he hears upon waking in the morning is the assistant boss of the gang next to him complaining that "the bastards" had shortchanged his gang one loaf of bread. A few minutes later the Tartar takes him away—not even for the misdemeanor of staying in bed but because a floor needs mopping. Shukhov is not surprised. It is to be assumed that every petty bureaucrat and minor official in the place (whether a prisoner or not) will take his cut from whatever pie is available. Almost any person with power or influence in the camp can be bribed. Nearly every manifestation of authority Shukhov encounters is tainted, and he survives in part because he recognizes this so clearly.

Nevertheless, in the face of this pervasive corruption and injustice, whenever Shukhov has more than an incidental contact with either an official or another prisoner, the reader gradually comes to realize that he is longing for a glimpse of old-fashioned humanity, some small light of honesty or decency or even purity and innocence shining through the facade of impersonality, skepticism, or belligerence that most everyone maintains. When he sloshes water under the warders' boots as he begins to mop their floor, Shukhov does not have high hopes for even a lukewarm personal contact (on the contrary, he wants to make short work of the job), and yet as the conversation unfolds, he does give the warders an opening. One of them says, "Didn't you ever see your old lady wash the floor, stupid?" Shukhov replies:

"They took me away from her in 1941, Comrade Warder. I don't even remember what she was like."

"Just look at how they mop. . . . The bastards can't do anything and don't want to either. They're not worth the bread we give 'em. They ought to get shit instead."

"Anyway, why mop the fucking thing every day? It makes the place damp all the time. Now, 854, listen here. Just wipe it over a little so it's not too wet and get the hell out of here."

. . . "Rice! You can't compare millet and rice!" . . . Shukhov quickly finished up the job (13–14).

It is probably true that he has forgotten his wife, but it is more true that had one of the warders asked, for instance, "You remember *nothing* about her?" Shukhov would have loved trying to remember. He is treated like a number, so he does the job like a number. These people are "dopes," he thinks, not "human beings" (14). His reaction is characteristically milder than Solzhenitsyn wants ours to be.

Despite the loud voices in this encounter, there is a quality of understatement which solicits the reader's indignation on Shukhov's behalf. These are bad men. Perhaps we can say that they are part of a system which spawns bullies and intimidators for its support, but these men are also bullies in their own right. They are enjoying their roles too much. As Alexander Schmemann has said,

Evil in Solzhenitsyn is real because it is always *personal*. It is not found in impersonal "systems" or "structures," it is always found in and caused by man. Even in the *sharashka* and in the cancer ward evil does not appear as some elemental force and fate to which man is absolutely subjugated and for which he is in no way responsible, and to which, after it is "explained" and "accepted," it remains only to stoically resign oneself. Above all and always, evil is *men* who have opted and continue to opt for evil, men who have truly chosen to serve evil.[4]

40

In his haste to make his major point Schmemann seems to overlook that there are certain inherited "structures" in Solzhenitsyn's world which make it *easier* for some men to choose evil, and perhaps he also forgets that Solzhenitsyn is a master at showing men who serve evil without quite knowing they do; but in the main Schmemann is right: In the end the blame falls on men, not systems. Almost always Solzhenitsyn's best men, like Gleb Nerzhin in *The First Circle*, choose simply not to serve the system (at whatever cost to themselves).

Not long after Shukhov leaves these two evil warders, he tries to get admitted into the hospital, but the young medic (and poet and prisoner) Vdovushkin finds that his temperature is just under ninety-nine.

> "If it were over a hundred. it'd be a clear case. But as things are I can't let you off. Take a chance and stay if you want. If the doctor takes a look at you and thinks you're sick. he'll let you off. But if not, it's the cooler for you. You'd be better off going to work." (24–25)

Vdovushkin does not seem so bad. He is not exactly sympathetic to Shukhov, but neither is he hostile. Because we are afforded several quick glimpses into his mind (when he must, Solzhenitsyn switches point of view in *Ivan Denisovich* without blinking, an early example of the so-called "polyphonic" technique which he uses so often in later novels), we learn that he knows Shukhov "was not one of those who's always hanging around the hospital block" and so he takes him seriously—not as an "individual" but as a patient. When Shukhov entered the hospital, Vdovushkin spoke abruptly but thrust a thermometer into his mouth nevertheless (he could have thrown him out immediately) and went back to writing his poetry. Now when Vdovushkin refuses him, Shukhov

> didn't even nod. He rammed on his cap and went out.

When you're cold, don't expect sympathy from someone who's warm (25).

Compared to Shukhov's response to the warders, this
seems excessively angry, and we wonder if Vdovushkin
deserves it. Now Shukhov is whining more than we would
like.

Vdovushkin, however, like all the intellectuals in *Ivan
Denisovich*, is guilty of bland indifference toward men
like Shukhov, and the irony is that men like Shukhov are
much more alive and interesting than the intellectuals.
(Things change on this score when we get to *The First
Circle*.) If Vdovushkin were a real poet, he would look
Shukhov in the eye, ask questions, learn something; he
would look at the man, not squint at the thermometer.
The person Vdovushkin most admires—his patron and
boss, the doctor Stepan Grigoryevich—is regarded by
Shukhov as "a loudmouth know-it-all" (23), and we are
to see that the doctor's ideas are purely theoretical.
Vdovushkin himself seems overly committed to the rules
and regulations of the bureaucracy (in a sense, it supports
his writing of poetry), and he is not a qualified medic,
either; he "started learning how to give injections to poor,
ignorant prisoners who would never let it enter their
simple, trusting minds that a medic might not be a medic
at all" (24). Such a condescending attitude *is* stupid and
wrong, and although Vdovushkin, unlike the warders,
does not seem beyond redemption, he comes close to
being so. As a student of literature, he should know better.

A few pages later, we come to the scene where another
man of ideas, Caesar, is smoking, "thinking about something" (32), while Shukhov and Fetyukov wait and worry
about who gets the butt. Although there is irony in his
portrait (he "smoked to help his mind come up with great
ideas" [33]), Caesar at least has taken the men seriously
enough to know the character of each, and his gift of the
butt to Shukhov implies that a discrimination between
them has been made (notwithstanding the fact that Caesar

may regard Shukhov as useful). Caesar is no bundle of warmth, but he is a better man than Vdovushkin.

In between the abortive hospital visit and this incident with Caesar, Shukhov goes to Pavlo, the assistant gang boss, for his bread ration; Pavlo inquires, "Didn't they put you in the cooler, Ivan Denisovich? And are you still alive?" (26), and Shukhov rather casually notes Pavlo's Western Ukrainian politeness. But that politeness counts for something. Shukhov is polite in return, though not unaware that Pavlo is "a big shot of sorts." Shukhov then hurries away to check his ration. Pavlo's attentiveness tells us, however, that he is a good man, one of the best we have met so far in this novel.

Let me repeat that Solzhenitsyn's ideal reader is one who makes such judgments, charts Shukhov's moral and ethical behavior, and casts a cold eye on every character in the novel. The reader's judgment may often differ from Shukhov's, but he is asked to exercise it, not to remain a tolerant or detached observer. After only a few pages of this or any Solzhenitsyn work we know that in his opinion one of the curses of our time is the weakness and relativity of most men's sense of right and wrong, their reluctance to pass moral judgment, their willingness to tolerate anything. Solzhenitsyn is always sensitive to small things of real value; he prizes unexpected kindnesses and tiny gifts of goodwill passing between people, and he expects us to do so as well. We remain on watch for small-scale outbreaks of goodness. Large goodness we don't expect in this barren prison camp. There are no authentic priests or saviors here. We are looking for mediators of humanity, not divinity, some bit of evidence that even here in this last circle of hell all is not yet lost.

The visible rule of the shrewder prisoners like Shukhov is that it is every man for himself; and yet the novel has many incidents where one may see the possibility (and sometimes the realization) of old-fashioned Christian charity—self-sacrifice rather than selfishness. If part of the reading experience of *Ivan Denisovich* is watching how Shukhov maintains himself with some dignity and balance, another part of that experience is seeing if he can keep from swallowing whole the every-man-for-him-self rule. Bad men often keep their dignity and balance; we want Shukhov to do more than that; we want him to be better than he is.

At the noon meal break the moral and ethical issues facing Shukhov become somewhat more complicated than earlier. Because food is the first requirement for survival, meals are the most important events of the day, the mess hall the most important institution in the camp. Mealtime is an occasion for the fittest among the prisoners to display their talent and their morality; it is a test, an interval packed with unpleasant tension, grotesque excitement, and a heightened awareness on the part of the characters, as if they are about to commit murder.

We are introduced to the mess hall by way of a long explanation of how every member of the mess hall hierarchy takes his cut from the available supply of food and always at the expense of the common prisoners; they "stole all the way down the line" (83). How maddening and demoralizing it must be for new prisoners to discover that even the meager, barely life-sustaining portion of food which is rightfully theirs is not safe from the pilferers. It is not just that the pilferers are hungry, too; they are also greedy and selfish; the camp is loaded with fat cooks, well-fed sanitary inspectors who don't inspect, and healthy trustees. Many people are taking advantage of others, and not because they have to. The idea of taking only your fair share is, with rare exceptions, bankrupt in this camp—and in Soviet society generally, and probably in the world at large. Shukhov has long ago realized this, yet he still complains about it, which is important. He himself is fairer than most.

The majority of common prisoners are forced to grovel like animals in order to get enough to eat. As the moment approaches when the bowls of gruel are distributed, the pushing, shoving, and grabbing are dismayingly furious and chaotic, yet throughout this scene Shukhov, Pavlo, and Gopchik are in control and work like a team to get the best for their gang. So despite the every-man-for-himself refrain echoing over the entire meal break, and despite Pavlo and Shukhov having "pushed their way through" (83) to the mess hall and Shukhov having chased away a couple of "goners" to get a table, it is not a case of every man for himself. It is every gang for itself, at least at the critical moment of mealtime. An unexpected bond between the members of the gang appears, and it works. Shukhov deceives the cook into giving the gang two extra bowls of gruel, and when he sees the two Estonians coming through the crowd, he slips the bowls to them.

The locations of stoves and warm spots are always known by the prisoners; so is the location of one's own gang—it is a point of reference and the only unit within which Shukhov can feel (relatively) safe and to which he acknowledges an allegiance. There is hate and envy among the gang members, but they also know and keep watch on each other; Shukhov's criticisms of Caesar and Fetyukov (or his praise of other gang members) is personal, based on intimate biographical knowledge; Shukhov is contemptuous of Fetyukov, but that is better even for Fetyukov than stony indifference. When Shukhov is called "S-854" by a guard or a warder, you feel a chill; when as a gang member he is called "Ivan Denisovich," you feel identity being preserved and are reminded that he is a recognizable person, very important facts when the entire weight of the camp and the waste of his days conspire to render him a nonentity. Within the gang he has a place and a role, and at the noon meal break he works hard for more than merely himself.

Nevertheless, he does work for himself, too. Because he has managed to get two extra bowls for his gang, he knows that his "cut" should be one of those bowls. But even "though it was Shukhov who'd finagled the bowls, it was Pavlo who doled them out" (89), and so he has to wait until Pavlo says, "Ivan Denisovich, take one for yourself," a statement which acknowledges the code of

45

fairness operating within the gang (as well as revealing yet another hierarchy). Among veterans like Pavlo and Shukhov nothing needs to be said; an impatient gesture or a hungry stare on Shukhov's part would be an unmanning vulgarity, perhaps an insult, and yet as he waits for Pavlo to give him the extra bowl he is stubbornly aware of his rights in the matter. One of Shukhov's consistently less likable traits is that he always knows what's coming to him. But as I have said before, he is far from a paragon and closer to a man who when he is "good" seems almost unconscious of that fact.

Shukhov gets his extra bowl at last; he takes

> his time over it, and he didn't even feel it when fellows from the new gang coming in pushed him. The only thing that worried him was Fetyukov might get an extra helping (90).

Another more or less peaceful moment is marred by Fetyukov, who always stimulates ungenerous feelings in others. Shukhov then notices that the Captain has finished his mush and is sitting alone, placidly unaware that the gang has acquired two extra bowls. Shukhov takes a perverse satisfaction in noticing how the Captain is still a camp innocent, a fairly recent arrival whose life will be changed by camp far more than he can possibly imagine at the moment. Suddenly Pavlo calls to the Captain and gives him the extra bowl:

> The Captain had a kind of shamefaced smile on his chapped lips. (He'd sailed ships all around Europe and the Arctic.) He bent down over the half bowl of thin oatmeal mush and he was happy (91).

Solzhenitsyn seems unable to resist giving repeated instances of once proud men who are now content with a little gruel, but in this case the Captain's unawareness and gratitude make him a worthy recipient of the extra bowl. He is not a Fetyukov. According to Shukhov and

46

the every-man-for-himself rule, the Captain will not survive unless he learns how to be cagey and selfish, and yet the novel also demonstrates that not all men are turned into selfish animals, either. Pavlo certainly isn't; neither is Shukhov. It is as if Solzhenitsyn wants us at first to agree that, yes, the camp forces men to live like animals but then to notice that, no, they do not all sacrifice their identity to sheer instinctive behavior. They have to talk tough, harden their skulls, prepare for the worst, but when they can safely be generous, the good ones are. Their humanity is narrowly confined by their need, but it is not vanquished utterly.

Pavlo helps the Captain along, and once Shukhov sees what Pavlo has done, he agrees that "it was only right." Pavlo is a degree or two more generous here than Shukhov (who for a moment thought he could get *both* extra bowls), but that seems consistent with Solzhenitsyn's view of Shukhov as a kind of average man in all respects. A fully sensitive Ivan Denisovich could mean a sentimental novel. He is not high enough in the gang's hierarchy to have the luxury of being generous without a motive, but he has an open disposition, he is capable of learning, and he sees immediately that Pavlo's action with the Captain is correct. Shukhov leaves the meal break with a full stomach, a sense of accomplishment, and the knowledge that he has done right by his peers. He was not as selfish as he could have been, and he lost no dignity. Hundreds of such meal breaks have occurred before and hundreds more are to come and all of them are something of a test, but this particular one is especially successful for Shukhov.

I have said that in my opinion Shukhov is the most consistently alive of all Solzhenitsyn's main characters. We do not see the author pulling the strings nearly as openly in this novel as in, for example, *The First Circle*; his voice is usually muted, his hands mostly invisible, and Shukhov seems to live a life of his own. But one of several exceptions to this is the short scene following the meal break when Shukhov takes a bowl of mush to Caesar, who is sitting in the warm office having a discussion about art with K-123, "a scrawny old man who'd done twenty years." The old man's position is that "Too much art is no art at all" (94) and Caesar's is that "it's not *what* but *how* that matters in art," and the entire discussion is meant to be over Shukhov's head. We are uncomfortably reminded of his place: that of a simple peasant with a fairly good heart who hands over the mush and stands there "for just as long as was decent" hoping that Caesar "might give him a little tobacco." For a man like Shukhov there *are* more important things than art and, yes, perhaps we should be reminded of the limits of his education, and it is ironical that Caesar and the old man ignore him for the sake of a purely theoretical discussion, and it is clever of Solzhenitsyn to bring into his narrative this venerable debate about art and then undermine both positions—notwithstanding that the old man's position is close to Solzhenitsyn's own. When the old man eats his mush, its taste is "wasted on him" because he is too full of ideas. But the problem is that suddenly Shukhov seems a little too simple, too much the imprisoned rustic who must focus only on the hard facts of existence. In this scene, we see so much more than he sees that we become aware of Solzhenitsyn's manipulations, and Shukhov becomes embarrassing, a kind of cardboard Everypeasant who is too obviously used to point up a contrast. The same thing happens later when Shukhov asks the Captain questions about the moon.

In Solzhenitsyn's fiction most Soviet institutions are pictured as citadels of waste and corruption. These hideous bureaucracies are likely to be packed with demoralized workers and paranoid managers: featherbedders, malingerers, sadists, incompetents, toadies and officials are everywhere. Rarely is a man doing a piece of useful work and enjoying it as Shukhov does when he finally is able to lay his first brick after the noon meal break. Skillful and talented people are constantly being frustrated and broken, their skills and talents either going unused or being perverted and tainted by some illegitimate institutional pressure or some unimaginative bureaucratic thug. Only about one-tenth of *Ivan Denisovich* is devoted to the day's work—laying bricks on a wall in the power plant. While good reasons are given for the delay in getting started, it is also true that everything seems to conspire against real productivity, as opposed to the appearance of it. Shukhov wants to work. In *The Gulag Archipelago Two*, Solzhenitsyn asks, "How could Ivan Denisovich get through ten years if all he could do was curse his work day and night?"[5] Once the wall starts going up, he loses himself completely and even works overtime. "I encountered this strange phenomenon myself," says Solzhenitsyn, "suddenly you become absorbed in the work itself, irrespective of whether it is slave labor and offers you nothing" (*Gulag II*, 259). Shukhov forgets his illness and doesn't feel "the cold any more," a significant fact in a novel where sheer physical warmth is as precious as gruel. Because he works as hard as he does, he becomes "a sort of gang boss for a time" (111). Nevertheless, in order for his gang to get a few courses of brick laid, it has almost to fight for the opportunity. Material must be stolen from other areas of the construction site; Shukhov has to guard his own trowel; the gang must put up with the interruptions of Der, the building foreman, a prisoner himself but also a former Moscow minister—and therefore a man concerned about regulations, appearances, and decorum rather than the realities of the job at hand. Committed bureaucrats always hinder real work in Solzhenitsyn's world. When men like Shukhov are prevented from using their initiative, everyone loses.

But for a time his enthusiasm is so infectious that the whole gang is caught up in the enterprise and happily yields to his leadership. He directs his gang in the details of bricklaying as if he is conducting a symphony. He thinks of the wall as his very own, he lays his bricks without a mistake, and at the end of the working day he appraises his achievement:

Not bad. He went up and looked over the wall from left to right. His eye was true as a level. The wall was straight as a die. His hands were still good for something! (125)

A man who can feel this is hardly a prisoner, and that is why the prison establishment sees to it that the situation does not last. Men who work this well and feel so good about it are dangerous. They become little whirlwinds of power and influence. Even though the official business of the prisoners is to build the power plant, and even though hundreds of eyes are watching to see that it is done, one senses that truly valuable and productive men like Shukhov have no place here. It is a world where incompetence, thievery, sloth, and cruelty are assumed, and it is unprepared for bursts of pure efficiency born of genuine enthusiasm, as happens in Shukhov's gang this afternoon. Again and again we learn that more depends "on the work rates than on the work itself" (68). As in any bureaucratic organization where people are trying to conceal their ineptitude, if news got out that Gang 154 had really achieved something important in a short time and against considerable odds, some people would hold the achievement against them—and it would surely be a commentary on how little the prison camp as a whole accomplishes.

At the end of the working day, Shukhov doesn't even know whether tomorrow he will be on this or another job, and he must hide his trowel if he ever expects to see it again. If productivity is the goal, it is astonishingly stupid that there is no way to identify Gang 154 and let them continue the job to its conclusion. But it is obvious here and elsewhere in Solzhenitsyn that most institutional projects limp along lamely, two steps backward for every step forward, and that most of the managers, officials, and supervisors put their energy into watching others, forming lines, seeing to it that no one steps out of those lines. Work gets done, but poorly and slowly.[6] On this day the brief interval of wall-building stands as a green island of freedom and improvisation, where progress is made by men left to themselves, but it is surrounded by a wasteland of gray hours in which these same men are managed by others—marched, prepared to march, frisked, counted off. This happens not only because this is a prison in the Soviet Union. The whole world is crowded with people who love to manage other people; it is hard to resist the opportunity to become a manager, even if you yourself were once among the managed. The building foreman Der has everything he wants, but he still "couldn't help throwing his weight around and acting smart" (118). The very highest authorities know and depend upon the fact that the next highest in authority—and so on down the line— will take exquisite pleasure in bullying and intimidating others as long as they themselves are in a safe position.

Although a good worker, Shukhov is not in love with just any kind of work for its own sake, nor is he especially interested in helping to build modern Russia. He knows that in the last analysis he is working for his food, and he knows that few people really care about the quality of the job, and Solzhenitsyn is probably being ironical in having a peasant who is comfortable with the old ways and "old sayings" employed in the construction of a power plant. But "bricklaying was a job you could take pride in" (72), and that's the point. Despite Solzhenitsyn's remarkable knowledge of science and technology, he again and again invests authority in characters like Shukhov whose sensibility and skills are essentially anachronistic. Shukhov's own children hope to attend technical school, and his own wife hopes to get a job making imitation carpets. Basket-weaving, carpentry, even working in one's own village— things for which Shukhov has an affection—all are nearly obsolete, and more than once it occurs to him that perhaps he is better off in prison than in the modern world.

Shukhov does not want to leave the brick wall. When it comes time to prepare for the march back to camp, he lingers over that wall, even to the extent of keeping all the other prisoners waiting. They start "screaming murder" at him. But almost the moment he hurries to join them, the tone of the novel changes back to what it was before the wall-building scene, as Shukhov has to concern himself again with details of his own survival and with how to get an edge on his immediate future. He has had the pleasure and luxury of losing himself; now he must watch himself. At work he had been a man and a leader of men, but as soon as he leaves work, he undergoes a series of diminishings: his fellow prisoners scream at him for being late; Solzhenitsyn has him ask silly questions of the Captain about the moon and the stars; he gets very cold; he joins in the verbal abuse of the Moldavian; his column finds itself racing the other column from the tool works back to camp, and although Shukhov's column wins, it "was like a bunch of scared rabbits gloating over another bunch of scared rabbits" (145). He is frisked; he stands in the package line for Caesar in hopes that Caesar will give him a reward; and at dinner he knocks away a man smaller than himself to get at a tray. He must stay alert. He cannot relax. He has moved back into prison camp time.

Official prison camp time shows itself in commands like "Snap out of it, 104! Out-si-ide!" or "Line up by fi-i-ves," the inevitability of which provides a kind of ghastly security for the prisoners. But in *Ivan Denisovich* there is also another time schedule, unofficial and private, measured in minutes seized in spite of the official schedule and pre-programmed routine. They are the precious parts of the day, and there is no mystery about when they occur: there is "that short, blissful moment" just before morning roll-call "when there was no way out any more, but people kidded themselves that there was" (25); the "best moment" comes just after the prisoners enter the construction site and the bosses leave them alone for a minute (52); and at dinner, as the gruel begins to reach their stomachs, this "was what a prisoner lived for, this one little moment" (169). Anticipating such moments is one of the ways a man keeps going, one of the ways he manages to stay alive in prison. Now and then Shukhov steals a few minutes—today he gets five extra in the infirmary —and he imagines that it would be heaven to have a stretch of time to himself. His "one dream" is to spend "three weeks without moving" in the hospital.

If Shukhov had three hours a day to himself, would prison be less hellish for him? I wonder. Even today when he has those extra minutes in the infirmary, he feels "odd" and begins to fidget—he studies the wall, he looks at his jacket, he touches his beard. Unlike the Captain, Caesar, and Alyoshka-the-Baptist, he does not have enough subjects in his head to carry on a discussion during periods of slack time or to stay interesting to himself alone. Although he is not stupid, he is unconscious of his own wisdom, which is the wisdom of the practical man—the worker, the doer. He needs to keep busy. Despite the many instances in the novel when he sucks all he possibly can out of a moment, when he savors his "free" time as if only he knows its full value, too many of these moments would debilitate him.

This is not to claim that he is better off in prison (he is wrong even when he tries to believe this himself), but he *has* adjusted to it, a fact which is both inspiring (because he gets so much out of so little) and shocking (because we may want him to be an indignant critic of the Soviet Union or man's inhumanity to man). One of the things you really must do in prison, and probably everywhere else, is find a way not to think of the time you have left. If a man knows the proper values, has a few skills, and manages to keep his health, his only other task in order to survive is to control his imagination so that at the end of the day he can say:

Nothing had spoiled the day and it had been almost happy. There were three thousand six hundred and fifty-three days like this in his sentence, from reveille to lights out.

The three extra ones were because of the leap years.

53

However, the addition of those last two sentences, the final two sentences of the novel, changes everything. It is as if a part of Shukhov's mind of which we have seen little suddenly breaks through, a part which counts the days, has nightmares, and is terrified. But even though the novel ends on this note, the counter-of-days is not the essential Shukhov, only an irrepressible part of him which we see when his defenses must be withdrawn if he is to cross the border to sleep. The weight of the entire novel is balanced against these last lines, as though Shukhov tries everything within his powers to fend off this idea, but finally, just before unconsciousness, at the margin of his self, the idea forces its way out, the idea of freedom. Despite everything, despite all his adjustments and skills and victories, he wants to be free, simply that. Nothing more. Free.

Probably his greatest victory in the course of the day is to keep that idea at bay. To become a counter-of-days in the course of a day would be to live in a prison within a prison. At one point in *Ivan Denisovich* we learn that you have to keep "your eyes on the ground" (76), which is a way of saying keep your eyes on the present, which in turn is the easiest advice ever conceived by the mind of a man and the most difficult to follow. Shukhov has a method of looking always a few feet ahead, of making short-term plans and creating obligations and worries for himself, so that part of his attention is focused not on the ground, nor on the distant future, but on the foreground. Will someone steal his trowel? Will his bread still be in his bunk when he returns? He worries about whether Caesar will receive a package in the mail, and he plans ahead so that he can stand in line for him. He keeps in the back of his mind his need to see the Latvian tonight about tobacco. He wonders what he will do with the piece of metal, which, risking his life, he smuggles back into camp. In fact, with the notable exception of the wall-building interval, from the novel's very opening scene, where Shukhov is in bed wondering about going to the infirmary, to the very last scene, where he is anticipating

54

what he will eat before roll call the next morning, he keeps his mind full of self-generated concerns—and as trivial as they often seem, they are not demoralizing or deadening in the way that counting the days is. Long, long thoughts of some future happiness are not his concern. He is a wise man.

He is not, however, as wise as the old man with the ramrod-straight back and worn wooden spoon whom he observes at supper. This old man is the first of a steady stream of characters Shukhov encounters in the evening and against whom, it seems, his own sensibility and knowledge are being measured. Shukhov admires the old man for never giving in, for being a pillar of dignity, for taking his time over his gruel and not allowing his eyes to shift around while he eats. Shukhov himself, as knowledgeable as he is, is a long way from achieving that kind of composure, and he knows it. Although he eats his supper with the care and deliberation of a watchmaker, the instant he finishes he pushes his metal spoon into his boot, jams his cap on his head, and takes off, ready to visit the Latvian and his store of tobacco. When he hurries away to conduct his affairs, he is doing what is necessary for him at this stage of his development, but it is as if the old man is further up the road, waiting for the Shukhovs to step off the treadmill. We do not know precisely how the old man has arrived at that stately position, but his face seems "hewed out of stone," dirt has worked itself into his hands, his spoon is worn and wooden, he is neat as a pin. He looms over the novel like an elder; he has authority; he is a superior man.

Shukhov next goes to the Latvian and barters with him as an equal. Each eyes the other, matching wits and intelligence, and we see again how skillfully Shukhov manages his life. But maybe we also feel that he is almost too shrewd a bargainer. The old man of the previous scene would have held himself apart from such a mundane exchange, not out of snobbery but from acquired wisdom. Shukhov is a bit uncomfortable in the presence of the old man, but he is at home with the Latvian—even though he must leave him quickly to return to his own barracks to witness Caesar opening his package.

When Caesar spreads his goods out on the lower bunk, the aroma of the foodstuffs wafting around the room, Shukhov manages to restrain himself as usual, to remind himself again that he is no scavenger and to conduct himself with the kind of dignity we have come to expect. His poise pays off: Caesar gives him his bread ration, and Shukhov knows himself well enough to reflect:

> Caesar's gruel and now his six ounces of bread—that was a whole extra supper—and this, of course, was as much as he could hope to make on that package. And he stopped thinking right away that he might get any of this fancy stuff and he shut it out of his mind. It was no good aggravating your belly for nothing. He had his own ten ounces of bread and now this ration of Caesar's and then there was that hunk of bread in the mattress. That was more than enough! (179)

Again we see the irony in Shukhov's settling for so little, but beyond the irony is the message: Not every man can find cause to celebrate over a little extra bread, not every man knows when he has more than enough. It is a message which cannot be repeated too often in Solzhenitsyn's work. It is not a celebration of poverty but rather of economy, reminiscent of the famous passage in *Walden*:

> I went to the woods because I wished to live deliberately, to front only the essential facts of life, and see if I could not learn what it had to teach, and not, when I came to die, discover that I had not lived. I did not wish to live what was not life, living is so dear; nor did I wish to practise resignation, unless it was quite necessary. I wanted to live deep and suck out all the marrow of life, to live so sturdily and Spartan-like as to put to rout all that was not life, to cut a broad swath and shave close, to drive life into a corner, and reduce it to its lowest terms. . . .

56

There is a vast difference between voluntary economy and enforced economy and between the "experiment" at Walden and Shukhov's forced interment in the prison, but both Thoreau and Solzhenitsyn are interested in showing men who in rather unpromising circumstances have learned to derive satisfaction from their lives.[7]

Let me hasten to add, however, that Shukhov has a way of seeming almost *too* content with his carefully erned position. After Caesar wills him the bread, Shukhov thinks about envying Caesar, but then reminds himself of all the problems wealth brings and all the people one has to pay off in order to keep a portion of that wealth for oneself. His musings on wealth end with the paragraph:

> Some fellows always thought the grass was greener on the other side of the fence. Let them envy other people if they wanted to, but Shukhov knew what life was about. And he was not the kind who thought anybody owed him a living (180).

It is too pat. We want him to scream a little more; and that, again, is why those last lines in *Ivan Denisovich* are so important. They remind us that inside the well-adjusted Shukhov, from whom we are meant to learn so much, there is another man, not at all well-adjusted, from whom we can learn nothing.

The next character to pass in review in these final pages is Fetyukov, in tears, bloody, apparently beaten up while trying to scrounge food. He walks past all the gang members, climbs up on the bunk, and digs his face in the mattress. Shukhov thinks:

> You couldn't help feeling sorry for him if you thought about it. He'd never live out his time in the camp. He just didn't know how to do things right (181).

And that is the last we see of Fetyukov, whose behavior from beginning to end is presented to us as lamentably bad. Even the cruelty of the guards and the camp officials is more acceptable to the Shukhovs than the whining weakness of Fetyukov, whose total lack of dignity is a strangely threatening and annoying reminder to them all of how not to act. It is good of Shukhov to consider feeling sorry for Fetyukov, but it is perhaps surprising that his sympathy does not extend further, does not make him *do* something for Fetyukov. No one, apparently, will show Fetyukov how to do things "right." It seems a matter of character and, to some extent, a matter of style—you either have it or you don't, like a member of a club or fraternity. Fetyukov's haplessness may be worth our sympathy, but he won't receive much from Shukhov, who already has too many demands made on his.

The Captain enters the barracks right on Fetyukov's heels. Throughout the day he has bumbled along, tried his best, made mistakes, talked loudly, and now is feeling proud of himself for having acquired some genuine tea. In a few minutes he will be taken off to the cooler as a result of an earlier transgression. Like Fetyukov, the Captain held an important position in his former life, but unlike Fetyukov there is something about the Captain which suggests that eventually he will learn to do things "right." He will learn without yielding up his manhood and fight back without being broken. Because this quality is obvious to the others, they are willing to help the Captain now, when he still needs help, in a way that they will not help Fetyukov, who presumably will be left to die on his own. They like the Captain; they don't like Fetyukov. That's the way life is, Solzhenitsyn seems to suggest.

But the last word is yet to come. In the final few pages of the novel, while Shukhov keeps one eye on Caesar and continues to calculate his own position in relation to the others and to count his achievements for the day, his other eye is on Alyoshka-the-Baptist. Even though he must keep his copy of the gospel well-hidden, Alyoshka appears to be the novel's Christian spokesman. Some time ago Alexander Schmemann called Solzhenitsyn "a Christian writer," and Solzhenitsyn promptly expressed his gratitude to Father Schmemann for explaining him to himself.[8] It is clear from Solzhenitsyn's writing elsewhere that he has always had sympathy for the Christian view of the world, and so it is tempting to say that Alyoshka-the-Baptist gets the last word because he lends a spiritual dimension to the book which Solzhenitsyn himself advocates and which justifies the optimistic tone at the end—otherwise we might think that Shukhov is happy only because his stomach is full. But such an explanation ties everything up into a far neater package than we actually have. As John Dunlop recently pointed out, because Solzhenitsyn lacks theological training and sophistication he tends to formulate his Christian beliefs "with an awkwardness more recalling Tolstoy's gropings than Dostoevsky's luminous soarings."[9]

It has never occurred to Shukhov not to believe in God, but neither has he really thought his religion through, and he continues his practice of asking Alyoshka simpleminded questions about God and prayer. Like lots of people, he disapproves of corrupt priests, he doesn't believe in heaven and hell, and he has had unfortunate experiences with other so-called Christians, but he also has a rock-bottom faith that God is alive. Even though Alyoshka informs Shukhov of the proper way to pray and is able to state the correct Christian position on a number of issues, Shukhov comes off as the better man, the better-balanced man. Though not bad, Aloyshka does seem ineffective, and his pure but extreme brand of Christianity comes a little too easy ("Rejoice that you are in prison," he says. "Here you can think of your soul" [198]). Alyoshka is a word man, a spokesman, whereas Shukhov is a Christian in spite of himself. When he gives Alyoshka a cookie on the next-to-the-last page of the novel, that action speaks louder than words and is followed by the reflection, "he didn't have very much but *he* could always earn something" (202). He may not be a Christian theorist, but he is capable of earning his own way and giving to others at the same time.

It is as if Alyoshka and his creed have been dispensed with rather abruptly, as if Shukhov himself, although he does not talk about it, is somehow a truer Christian than the Baptist spokesman. And even though Shukhov has treated a number of people badly, including Fetyukov and several "goners," we can probably accept that paradox in his character. His cheerfulness and optimism are based on a fundamental sense of security: There is a God, life has meaning, and as imperfect as he is, he will try to be as good as he can in a fallen world.

When Shukhov goes on to think about his day's successes, he attributes them to "luck," not to God as Alyoshka would, and in the last two paragraphs of *Ivan Denisovich* both Alyoshka and Christianity fade into the background. Shukhov focuses on the realities before him. He thinks about the juice in the meat he is chewing. He thinks about his piece of steel. He thinks about his wall. Then, suddenly at the very end, we have that voice which begins to count the days—a voice which keeps the reader from complacently deciding that Shukhov is content with the situation or has taken refuge in commonplace Christian formulas. Solzhenitsyn certainly wants us to think about a number of Alyoshka's ideas—as Shukhov says, the Baptist was "telling the truth." But the one thing wrong with Alyoshka is this: "You could tell by his voice and his eyes he was glad to be in prison" (199). In *Ivan Denisovich* that will not do.

A Note on *Ivan Denisovich* and *The Gulag Archipelago Two* (1975):

We should not forget that *Ivan Denisovich* is far from Solzhenitsyn's last word on the forced labor camps. The carefully measured and understated style, the predominately cheerful tone (irony notwithstanding), and Shukhov's spirited attitude could conceivably leave us with warm and happy feelings about the entire experience, as if it were exclusively a character-building enterprise, a blessing in disguise for some men, and not a forced labor camp at all. *Gulag II* gives a broader picture. Here, for example, is an excerpt from Solzhenitsyn's account of his own experience in the clay pits at the Novy Iyerusalim Camp:

And in the mess hall two kerosene lamps burned next to the serving window. And you could not read the slogan, nor see the double portion of nettle gruel in the bowl, and you sucked it down with your lips by feel.

And tomorrow would be the same and every day: six cars of red clay—three scoops of black gruel. In prison, too, we seemed to have grown weak, but here it went much faster. There was already a ringing in the head. That pleasant weakness, in which it is easier to give in than to fight back, kept coming closer.

And in the barracks—total darkness. We lay there dressed in everything wet on everything bare, and it seemed it was warmer not to take anything off—like a poultice.

Open eyes looked at the black ceiling, at the black heavens.

Good Lord! Good Lord! Beneath the shells and the bombs I begged you to preserve my life. And now I beg you, please send me death (197).

This tone we do not find in *Ivan Denisovich*.

CHAPTER TWO

The First Circle

The First Circle is more ambitious than *Ivan Deniso-vich*, many times longer, and has a much greater diversity of people, ideas, and situations. It is an encyclopedia of viewpoints, a cornucopia of information, an obviously important book. And yet artistically it is not as successful as *Ivan Denisovich*. In the latter, Shukhov seems consistently a real person in a real world, and we forget that the novel was written by the hand of man. In *The First Circle*, we can almost never forget that distracting fact. *The First Circle* has too many dead characters and flat spots; it is much too long and fragmented; it is hard to follow—even when it is re-read, which it must be. Nevertheless, many of its characters do live a far richer emotional and intellectual life than Shukhov and his associates, and there are some magnificent sections, better than anything in *Ivan Denisovich*: Gleb Nerzhin's visit with his wife Nadya, the story of "Mrs. R's" visit to the Butyrskaya prison, Innokenty Volodin's arrest and his first impressions of the Lubyanka, and many others, some of which I will discuss in this chapter. But as a whole *The First Circle* has the effect of buffeting its reader about among its characters, and not because that reader finds himself in a crowded, vital novelistic world but because he cannot be consistently engaged in that world. It is a book easier to study than to read.

Other commentators think differently, however. Georg Lukács regards *Ivan Denisovich* as merely preparatory for both *The First Circle* and *Cancer Ward*, which to him represent "a new high point in contemporary world literature." Both novels, says Lukács, are of a "new type," invented by Thomas Mann, in which "the very absence of a unified plot results in a highly dynamic narrative and in an internal drama."[1] Giovanni Grazzini believes that part of the fascination of *The First Circle* "lies in its brilliantly articulate structure, the way in which episodes of fear and cruelty lead harmoniously into elegiac moments. . . ." Never before, claims Grazzini, has the "genre of the polyphonic novel ('in which each character becomes the protagonist when the action concerns him,' as Solzhenitsyn explains) attained such complete artistic maturity. . . ."[2] But in my opinion the structure fails to deliver what it seems to promise. It frequently leads to dead ends, and too often the episodes of fear and cruelty are so obviously, so didactically, juxtaposed with the elegiac moments that the reader feels he is being underrated.

Solzhenitsyn tries to do too much in *The First Circle*, far more than he needs to. In his attempt to draw characters who come from practically every walk of life, who have a variety of opinions on many subjects, and whose personal biographies are bound to be news to us, Solzhenitsyn elicits our interest in more ideas and characters than we can accommodate—elicits our interest but then too often drops the character, so that when he reappears dozens or hundreds of pages later, we can hardly remember who he was. Except in the cases of Gleb Nerzhin, Lev Rubin, Dmitri Sologdin, and perhaps Innokenty Volodin,

63

Solzhenitsyn himself appears to lose interest in certain characters, including most of the women and many of the lower-echelon guards, just when they begin to come alive, and he allows them to become representatives of stock attitudes or harden into stereotypes. After a meticulous introduction, a character's subsequent appearances may be so brief or one-dimensional that we wonder what happened to Solzhenitsyn's earlier investment in him. The novel should either be a thousand pages longer, to allow space for all those promising characters to develop, or two hundred pages shorter. Dozens of editorial and explanatory passages, several entire chapters, and a few characters could be crossed out without any loss. The best parts of this novel show a disciplined imagination at work, but many other sections seem disorderly, as if Solzhenitsyn felt time was running out and wanted to cram in as much as possible.

In theory a successful polyphonic novel reveals an entire society through a number of equally engaging points of view. "Each character," says Solzhenitsyn, "becomes the central one while he is in the field of action. The author must thus speak through thirty-five heroes. He should not give preference to any one of them. He must understand and motivate all his characters."[3] Georg Lukács finds this the perfect form for writers portraying socialist reality, but it runs the risk of working against that old inclination of habitual novel readers to identify with one or two main characters rather than spread their sympathies too thinly. It won't do to dismiss that inclination as a mark of the reader's bourgeois individualism, either (even though most Americans would probably not object to the label). The notion that the author should not give, or can refrain from giving, preference to any one of his heroes is misleading. Whether the author intends it or not, among those thirty-five heroes some are going to live lives of their own and seize our attention, make us miss them when they are absent, and make the other characters seem dull by comparison. Such an artificial theory of equality imposes a severe restraint on the author, and it may in fact explain why several figures in this novel seem to have had the life pruned out of them. Possibly Solzhenitsyn was overly committed to the theory of the polyphonic novel, although there is little reason to suspect that he is especially interested in novel "theory" at all. In an effort to approach his subject from all angles, in his urgency to tell *all* there is to tell, he uses many characters and many points of view. Sometimes this works, but more often in *The First Circle* it seems an arbitrary and self-indulgent technique. In any case, two main characters do emerge, but because so many other voices are vying for our attention, too, when we return to Gleb or Lev it is with relief, as if with them we can comfortably regain our bearings. This is surely not what Solzhenitsyn intended. One assumes that he wanted each of his characters to make a separate and distinct impression in our minds and for us to leave the novel feeling that it was a successful orchestration, during which we forgot the orchestra leader. That does not happen.

On the other hand, no novel is flawless. Most readers of novels have patience, and much in *The First Circle* is worth waiting for. With the exception of *Cancer Ward*, no contemporary Russian novel available to American readers can yield as much information about how Russians today live their lives. That is reason enough to read it. In the past, because we knew so little about the Soviet Union, those who knew a bit more—the Kremlin watchers, the social scientists and historians, the editors of *Soviet Life*, the ideologues of the left and right—had us at their mercy, but page after page of *The First Circle* (and *Cancer Ward*) has precisely that quality of undramatized news about small things which so often in the past has made novels sourcebooks of their worlds. We discover that there are real people living in the Soviet Union. Furthermore, of course, Solzhenitsyn wants his readers to ponder deeper questions. As we read the novel we are frequently placed in the position of overhearing eloquent discussions about the meaning of life, about ideology, philosophy, and religion, about what Faulkner

65

called the "old verities and truths of the heart." That we are put in this position is embarrassing to some sophisticated readers, but whether we agree or not, Solzhenitsyn believes that literature is where you put serious matters—it is no place to receive mere esthetic bliss—and undeniably he gives us much to think about in *The First Circle*. Despite his didactic attempts to change our miseducated minds and hearts, as in the highly rhetorical concluding lines of nearly every chapter, it is refreshing to encounter a writer who still believes that he has an audience made up of serious people and who still believes that there is such a thing as a "world" literature, which communicates

the condensed experience of one region to another in such a way that we will cease to be split apart and our eyes will no longer be dazzled, the units of measurement on our scales of values will correspond to one another, and some peoples may come to know the true history of others accurately and concisely and with that perception and pain they would feel if they had experienced it themselves—and thus be protected from repeating the same errors.[4]

The First Circle begins at 4:05 P.M. on Saturday, December 24, 1949, when Innokenty Volodin, a young diplomat, makes a telephone call to warn a distinguished doctor (an old friend of his mother's) not to give a gift to foreigners lest he be arrested by the secret police. The novel ends less than 48 hours later, early on Monday morning, December 26. Innokenty is now in the Lubyanka prison, having been arrested for making that telephone call. Between the telephone call and the arrest are six hundred pages, and it is possible to regard the purpose of the novel to be to show how a bright and promising young man like Innokenty can end up in prison for the rest of his life because he obeyed the dictates of his conscience.

But the bulk of those six hundred pages is about the men who live and work at the Mavrino "sharashka," a special prison near Moscow which houses a scientific research institute composed mostly of imprisoned intellectuals and scientists. Here, compared to that in most prisons, the food and working conditions are good—it is only "the first circle" of hell. The men live in the Mavrino Prison, they work in the Mavrino Institute. Both establishments are on the same grounds, but each has a separate set of administrative officials. One of the Institute's projects is a mechanism for making voice prints, a mechanism which eventually helps to identify Innokenty Volodin. So it becomes evident that every person and event in the novel is somehow connected to the sharashka.

In Chapter 2 prisoners from other camps are being brought to Mavrino and they can hardly believe that things are going to be so nice here:

> "An ounce and a half of butter! Black bread—*out on the table!* They don't forbid books! You can shave yourself! The guards don't beat the zeks."[5]

The newcomers ask questions, the older residents of the sharashka reply, and out of the welter of anonymous voices, one voice, that of Lev Rubin, begins to assume an identity of its own.

In the next chapter we learn more about Rubin. He is an orthodox Communist and a Jew who in freedom was a philologist specializing in Germanic languages; during the war he was given the job of converting German POWs into Russian agents. He had come to love and pity the Germans, and for this he was arrested. On this particular evening we find him attending the Christmas celebration of the small German population at the sharashka. Within the chapter, the point of view shifts briefly into the minds of two of the Germans (one hates Rubin; the other loves him).

We follow Rubin into the acoustics laboratory, where he has a conversation with his best friend Gleb Nerzhin, and in the next chapter the conversation continues, but now we are with Nerzhin's point of view. Among the characters in *The First Circle*, Nerzhin is the one we get to know in depth. Many of the details of his life correspond to what is known of the author's own.

Unlike his friend Rubin, Nerzhin is not committed to the Soviet system. Although he has a wife in freedom, he is loved by Simochka, a free employee at the sharashka; she is actually a lieutenant in the MGB, but like all the female employees, she has learned that the prisoners are hardly the ferocious enemies of the state they have been made out to be. By training a mathematician, Gleb spends most of the time writing in a tiny hand on small sheets of paper. More than anything else, he is interested in "learning about life" (49) and inquiring into the facts of modern Russian history. Throughout these chapters other characters appear and reappear.

In Chapter 9 one of his former teachers comes to Mavrino to ask for Gleb's help on a special state project, but Gleb refuses even though it would mean a shortening of his term and having his "conviction" removed from his record. "Let them admit first," he says, "that it's not right to put people in prison for their way of thinking, and then *we* will decide whether we will forgive *them*" (50). The moment he declares this decision, Colonel Yakonov, the chief of the Mavrino Institute, writes on his desk pad: "Nerzhin to be sent away" (50).

By this point in the novel, it is clear that Solzhenitsyn wishes to fold into his narrative as many people and situations as he possibly can and to show the extent to which terror and intimidation is a part of Soviet life outside of prison as well as within prison. While the main plot line remains in abeyance, we receive several life stories, and we move in and out of various points of view. There is a brief history of the sharashka and of the roles played in that institution by Colonel Yakonov and by the prisoner Mamurin, a former associate of Beria who wields as much power in prison as he did in freedom. We are introduced to Ruska Doronin, an energetic twenty-three-year-old friend and protégée of Gleb Nerzhin who is infatuated with Clara Makarygin, another free employee

and ironically the daughter of state prosecutor Makarygin, the kind of man nearly all the zeks have reason to
hate. Depending on their own values and their usefulness
to whatever project they are engaged in, some of the
prisoner-scientists have better relationships than others
with prison officials and ranking members of the bureaucracy. Some prisoners, like Khorobrov, who had originally
been imprisoned for writing on his election ballot "crude
peasant curses directed against the Greatest Genius of
Geniuses" (62), are expendable—and so when he refuses to show the proper respect for Yakonov and Mamurin and for the project of Laboratory Number Seven he,
too, is sent away.

Chapters 15 and 21 take us out of the sharashka and
upwards into the Soviet hierarchy—all the way up to
Minister of State Security Abakumov and then to Stalin
himself. We see how a decision by Stalin—or some little
twitch in his temperament—has reverberations all the way
back down to the sharashka. After Stalin, we return to
Colonel Yakonov and learn of his life, his values, and of
his fear of being held responsible for the failure of various
Mavrino Institute projects.

Chapter 24 introduces Dmitri Sologdin, an eccentric,
bright, thirty-six-year-old designer who has spent twelve
years in prison. Unlike Colonel Yakonov, who feels himself being squeezed to death by bureaucratic processes,
Sologdin has found a number of ways to be his own man:
He saws wood, he speaks in a special language of his own,
the "language of maximum clarity," and he teaches
younger men like Gleb what he has learned from so
many years in prison.

Solzhenitsyn then writes of the jailers, the men who
run the prison part of Mavrino and who are in charge of
"security." There is Junior Lieutenant Nadelashin, a sur-
prisingly nice person, an "unusual person" (164) whose
secret passion is being a tailor, not a prison guard. There
is grim Senior Lieutenant Shusterman and cruel Major
Myshin, the chief security officer, and Lieutenant Colonel
Klimentiev, in command of them all, a man who does not

think himself a "bureaucratic clod" (176) but who nevertheless is just that. These men reappear from time to time later on.

In the next few chapters Solzhenitsyn examines with us the character of several prisoners. There is Potapov, a builder of the Dnieper Hydroelectric Power Station, once regarded as a "robot" by his friends but who turns out also to have a live conscience; and Khorobrov, the outspoken rebel who will soon be sent away along with Gleb Nerzhin; and Adamson, a supporter of the Soviet state despite all his years in prison. Throughout this section we are given details of daily life in prison and in the laboratory. We learn more about Sologdin: Because he has managed to keep a low profile in prison, he has been able to work alone, without pressure and harassment, and he consequently has succeeded in designing all by himself an "absolute encoder" (one of the sharashka's major projects). He could trade the design for his freedom— in fact, one of his old and much admired professors, Chelnov, urges him to do just that—but he is worried about the uses to which his invention would be put. Another problem for Sologdin, a master of self-discipline, is that he is being tempted by the sensual Larisa Emina, one of those "twenty-two wild, irrational women, free employees, who had been allowed into that somber building" and who "had found a secret attachment here, were in love with someone and embraced him in secret, or had taken pity on someone and put him in touch with his family" (231). Sologdin yields to Ermina and to his own long-repressed sexual desires.

Immediately after this, Lev Rubin is also put to a test: Will he allow his skill as a voice print expert to be used by the state? Yes. It is Rubin's work which will eventually identify Innokenty Volodin and lead to his arrest. At the very time Rubin decides to cooperate with the authorities, his best friend Nerzhin is preparing for a visit with his wife Nadya, a visit which is likely to be their last. Much of the middle section of *The First Circle* has to do with Gleb and Nadya's anticipation of this visit and with

Nadya's past and present life. She is a student and lives with a group of other women, each of whom we learn something about. Chapter 37 is devoted to Nadya visiting Gleb, and Chapter 38 to Natalya Gerasimovich, a woman of fifty, visiting her husband, a prisoner-physicist specializing in optics who later also will decide against using his talents for the sake of the state.

We see something of the daily lives of the two prisoners' wives. Then Solzhenitsyn devotes three chapters to the free worker Clara Makarykin and her budding love for the prisoner Ruska Doronin and the way of life of her fashionable family—her brother-in-law is the diplomat Innokenty, her father a famous state prosecutor. We return to the prison for Gleb Nerzhin's ruminations after having visited with his wife; and for the biography of Ruska, once on the All-Union list of criminals and now a free-spirited double agent who is hatching a plan to expose all the stool pigeons in camp. Then it is back outside again to the world of Nadya Nerzhin and her roommates. We also see the effect of the visit upon her, and we meet Captain Shchagov, an ex-soldier and admirer of hers.

Chapters 48 to 54 show how the prisoners spend Sunday evening, their only "free" time during the week: conversation, an impromptu play, a birthday party (for Gleb). We learn more about the "pure" Communist Adamson and the so-called "robot" Popatov. Other characters continue to reveal themselves. A story, "Buddha's Smile," is told of a UN inspection tour of the infamous Butyrskaya prison led by "Mrs. R." and how everything is arranged so that the Westerners leave singing the praises of the conditions there.

In ironic juxtaposition to the prisoners' Sunday evening at Mavrino, Chapters 55 to 59 are devoted to a Sunday evening dinner party at prosecutor Makarygin's; a group of fashionable Muscovites have gathered to celebrate his second award of the Order of Lenin. As at Mavrino, both trivial matters and important issues are discussed, and we see a social level we have not seen before in *The First*

71

Circle. When Innokenty Volodin telephones his wife at the party, the call is secretly recorded; Lev Rubin will listen to it the next morning at Mavrino. During this section we learn more about Innokenty and how he came to acquire a conscience. We also see the growing political awareness of Clara Makarygin. Prosecutor Makarygin is put on the defensive both by his daughter and by an old friend, Radovich, an old Marxist who remembers the prosecutor when he was not a prosecutor. The party is attended by a famous author and a famous critic, and through these figures Solzhenitsyn makes statements about the condition of Russian art and letters. Throughout the dinner party we should remember that Gleb Nerzhin as a prisoner helped to lay the parquet floor of this very apartment building.

Chapters 60 to 64 take us back to the sharashka. Sologdin and Rubin are arguing about the laws of dialectics, and the argument becomes increasingly heated. We are given more information about Gleb and his views regarding "simple working people" (450). We meet Spiridon, the janitor at Mavrino and a man whose "folk profundity" (454) has considerable appeal to Nerzhin. While vigorous discussions about good and evil and the meaning of life are taking place here, we are suddenly moved to Innokenty Volodin's apartment, where he is climbing into bed with his wife, Dotty. Back at Mavrino, while the others sleep, Lev Rubin is contemplating incidents from his past, including the murders he had committed while trying to collectivize a village. Chapter 68 is about Adam Roitman, Colonel Yakonov's deputy and rival at Mavrino, who lives in the apartment directly below prosecutor Makarygin. Roitman, once an anti-Semitic Jew, is worried about a new outbreak of anti-Semitism against himself, and he too has a guilty conscience over past crimes against others.

Chapter 69 begins a series of chapters dealing with the activities of various characters on Monday morning. We learn what motivates men like Major Shikin, the Institute's security officer, and Boris Stepanov, the Communist Party secretary at Mavrino, both of whom bully other members of the camp administration as well as the prisoners. Sologdin, whose design of the absolute encoder could take the pressure off Colonel Yakonov, cleverly arranges it so that the colonel will have to pay a price for that design. We are introduced to Arthur Siromakha, the king of the stool pigeons, and shown the whole network of informers in the camp. We see the interrogation technique of Major Myshin, the prison security officer. Major Shikin, Myshin's counterpart at the Institute, questions Spiridon about a damaged lathe and then has a run-in with Ruska Doronin.

Chapter 78 switches briefly to Innokenty Volodin, who feels the noose gradually tightening. Back at Mavrino, the prisoner Gerasimovich is asked to make a secret camera but refuses and seals his fate by declaring, "I don't set traps for human beings!" (538) Meanwhile, Lev Rubin has gone ahead with his voice print work, making it possible for the authorities to arrest Volodin.

Chapters 82 to 84 are devoted to the arrest and to Innokenty's first few hours in the Lubyanka. Back at Mavrino, Nerzhin and Khorobrov and Gerasimovich are preparing to leave for a lower circle of hell. Most of the prisoners we have seen before reappear in the last two chapters, and their characters are further revealed by their manner of saying farewell to Nerzhin. In the last chapter, the van comes. It is painted a "gay orange and blue" (673) and is labelled "Meat."

It takes about a hundred pages for the major issues to emerge from the cacophony of voices we hear at the beginning of *The First Circle*. Working in the Mavrino Institute are some of the most talented men in the Soviet Union, almost all of whom can see further than Ivan Denisovich Shukhov. To what extent will these men allow themselves and their talents to be used by the very system which imprisoned them? Can they help it? Why do some rebel? Why do some happily consent to serve an immoral and evil system? What keeps others from even seeing the immorality of it all? Throughout Solzhenitsyn's work, but most notably in *The Gulag Archipelago*, there is a voice claiming that no system of government can be called successful which has taken so many millions of lives. Indeed, where terror and intimidation are the primary means of motivating people, not much gets done, or done well. But the fact is that things *are* accomplished in the Soviet Union and millions of citizens there *do* believe the system is successful and are trying to make it more so. Many people do not feel terrorized or intimidated, especially some of those who do the terrorizing, and others feel it but also live with it without protest. In *The First Circle* Solzhenitsyn wants to account for that unpleasant truth. What motivates the prison guards and the bureaucrats whose job it is to keep others in line? What motivates the ministers of state? What motivates Stalin himself? Are these people all bad? Why do so many of those in freedom choose to ignore or to justify the reality of the prison camps? The heroes in *The First Circle* are those like Gleb Nerzhin, Khorobrov, and Gerasimovich—the men who refuse to sell out to the state for any price and hence remain forever buried in the camps—but equally interesting are those characters who are less than heroic, not all of whom are bad man.

Lev Rubin is the most instructive example of a good man who serves evil. He is a complicated character, more difficult to render than the heroes, whose justifications for their actions are far less elaborate (though more profound) than his. Solzhenitsyn knows that he cannot simply dismiss as conscienceless and evil all those who disagree with his own view of how life ought to be, and so he tries hard to understand Rubin before showing that, yes, finally, people like him have to share the blame for the continuation of the immoral Soviet state. One senses in reading *The First Circle* that practically every character within the sharashka is based on someone Solzhenitsyn actually knew during his own imprisonment, and none of them matters more to him than Lev Rubin. Rubin is civilized and tolerant; he loves people and has a forgiving heart; he befriends the Germans in camp even though he knows some hate him; he is talented, well-educated, clever, something of an actor, optimistic, a "good man" as Gleb says (20), a philologist, a teacher. Indeed, he is so much the good person, teacher, and scholar that he resembles a familiar type one might see on any college campus in the United States. He is charming, articulate, the "spokesman for progressive ideology in the sharashka" (441), and he has just enough self-doubt and guilt in him to temper his beliefs and make him seem worth listening to. There are any number of dull and dreary Communists in Solzhenitsyn's fiction, people who follow the party line because they lack imagination and intelligence, but Rubin is not one of them, and that is why Solzhenitsyn is so concerned about him. If Rubin and others like him believe that Stalin is "really wise" and "sees far beyond what we can possibly see" and that the "state can't exist without a well-organized penal system" (41), then Stalin and his methods have support among the best and the brightest, not just among the dull and the ordinary. How can that be?

David M. Halperin has said that Rubin

has his own "absolute truth"—the false religion of Marxism-Leninism which allows no other competing truth and no other objectivity. His is a collective, rather than a personal, moral system, rooted in the revealed "truth" about the flow of history. In his theory the Good is manifested by whatever and whoever represents the "progressive forces" of history.[6]

Similarly, Giovanni Grazzini says that to Rubin, "in his certainty of being in possession of the absolute, crystal-clear truth, the Communist ideology explains and justifies the whole of history, and he regards men's errors as dialectical elements in progress."[7] It is obvious that in the character of Rubin Solzhenitsyn wants to draw a complete portrait of a Marxist intellectual, and it is also obvious that Solzhenitsyn regards Rubin's views as oversimplified, wrong, and destructive. But there are further

75

questions. Why does Rubin believe as he does? And *does* he really believe it as religiously as he seems to? The answer to the last question is no, not quite. Toward the end of the novel when he feels seared "with a red-hot brand" (481), we see that he has a conscience even if he avoids using that term himself, and his "Project for Civil Temples" (Chapter 67) shows the extent of his dissatisfaction with things as they are. Throughout the novel, in countless small instances, we see his sense of humor, his ability to apprehend other people's points of view, and his humanity—his very tone suggests that his ideology is not always in the forefront of his mind. When Gleb Nerzhin interrupts one of Lev's passionate appreciations of literature with, "Oh, Lev, my friend, I love the way you are right now, when you argue from your heart and talk intelligently and don't try to pin abusive labels on things" (37), it is as if often in the past, in unguarded moments, Lev has thought and felt beyond ideology. But during those dramatic scenes in *The First Circle* when he is on stage or arguing, situations which can force one to take dogmatic positions, it is easy to believe that he would rather die than yield an ideological point—and perhaps he would, in spite of those unguarded moments when his "heart" shows through.

Rubin defends Marxism, communism, and Stalinism because he is attracted to programs which offer, as Joyce Cary puts it, a "clear picture."[8] He also needs to be loved, or at least to feel that he belongs; at one point in his past, "anxious to expiate his guilt in the eyes of the Komsomols, and to prove his usefulness both to himself and the revolutionary class," he went off to collectivize a village by force, and people died as a result (480–481). And he needs constant validation for a style of mind that one could call "academic," which loves to administrate and manipulate, which values systematic classifications, patterns, and the labelling of people and their positions and opinions according to some historical antecedent, as if it were not possible for a man to have a new perception. Lev feels he must *use* his excellent education. He can never hold it back. He is rarely silent, or puzzled. Although from time to time a personal emotion or a twinge of conscience *does* take him by surprise, in his official view of things there is little room for mystery or surprise. He seeks order, intellectual security, a solid foundation, a reference point. Marx and Stalin give him that. He is willing to overlook the hard fact of his own imprisonment so long as he can believe that in general his country is progressing toward wholeness. Prison itself is merely part of a network of viable and purposeful institutions. "Everyone," says Cary, "has

> noticed the self-confidence of the Marxist convert. The neurotic and frustrated muddle-head of a month ago, uncertain and bewildered in every contact, in every relation, has become completely sure of himself and full of eagerness to realise this world that he has now found, to realise himself, to enjoy himself in that world. That is why he is also indifferent to facts or argument. He does not accept any fact that would injure his new faith, in which alone he finds his way in life.
>
> This desire for the guide, the clear picture which sets free, is so urgent that almost any dogmatic statement, so long as it is simple and clear, will be accepted.[9]

Rubin, though not a muddle-head, is a lot like this. He wants the world to dovetail with his conceptual view of it. Many people have this craving for order. Except for the most perverse among us, people want to be in harmony with their world, and often they will lie to themselves to simulate harmony. That is what Rubin does. And we can understand his behavior and his thoughts. Any ideology promising happiness on this earth is hard to resist, and sometimes any means to that noble end seems justified. If things are not yet perfect, they soon will be. Rubin tirelessly tries to prove to his fellow prisoners that "according to comprehensive statistics and in the over-all view everything was going as it should, industry was flourishing, agriculture was producing a surplus, science was progressing by leaps and bounds, culture was shining like a rainbow" (476).

In Chapters 7 and 8 Rubin and Gleb Nerzhin discuss the nature of happiness. Gleb tells Rubin that in the labor camps he learned how to think, and he discovered that happiness depends not on how many "external blessings we have snatched from life" but on "our attitude toward them" (39); he uses as an example the process of eating gruel:

> "You eat it slowly; you eat it from the tip of the wooden spoon; you eat it absorbed entirely in the process of eating, in thinking about eating—and it spreads through your body like nectar. You tremble at the sweetness released from those overcooked little grains and the murky liquid they float in. And then—with hardly any nourishment—you go on living six months, twelve months. Can you really compare the crude devouring of a steak with this?" (38)

Thus is made explicit what was mostly implicit in *Ivan Denisovich* (many other passages in the first hundred pages of *The First Circle* read like a gloss on that book).[10] Rubin does not exactly agree with Gleb, but he is amused by his method of arriving at his conclusions. He calls him an "eclectic." He wonders where he "gets" his views. Then he accuses Gleb of preferring his own "personal experience to the collective experience of humanity" (40), which is partly true. A committed specialist himself, Rubin doesn't believe Gleb has the right to think for himself: "You're a mathematician, and you have no real knowledge of history and philosophy" (42). When Gleb laughs at Stalin, Rubin maintains that Stalin "sees far beyond what we can possibly see" (41). Gleb claims that every one of Stalin's thoughts "is crude and stupid" and calls on Rubin to "believe your own eyes" (41).

Both men are sincerely concerned about the fate of their fellow men and in this discussion they present their credentials as reliable witnesses to their worlds. Rubin believes that things must be seen in their "historical perspective"; Gleb believes that a single man, by trusting his instincts and opening his eyes, can see things as they "are" (and by extension as they have been and will be). Both men revere "history," but when Rubin speaks of "historical perspective" and "the collective experience of humanity" he is using what Solzhenitsyn wants us to notice is ideological jargon—comforting, ready-made terminology. He is not perceiving life as it is. Lev has thrust his education between himself and his world. His mind is overlaid with a conceptual crust, to borrow a phrase from Joyce Cary again. He is a victim of that kind of education which values the abstract generalization, "ideas," the classifying formula or label, and which puts most of its faith in specialists and experts. Cary died some years before Solzhenitsyn was first published, but near the end of his remarkable book on art and reality there is a passage which names what Solzhenitsyn also sees as a fundamental problem:

. . . after twenty-five, few people are open to new ideas on any subject—they are crusted over with a conceptual education which has entirely cut them off from the living world.

The concept, the label, is perpetually hiding from us all the nature of the real. We have to have conceptual knowledge to organise our societies, to save our own lives, to lay down general ends for conduct, to engage in any activity at all, but that knowledge, like the walls we put up to keep out the weather, shuts out the real world and the sky. It is a narrow little house which becomes a prison to those who can't get out of it.

The artist, the writer, simply in order to give his realisation, his truth, has to break these walls, the conceptual crust.[11]

It is significant that Gleb Nerzhin has become a writer of "needle-small notes" (31), one-man records of personal views and private judgments—this despite all those bureaucratic and ideological pressures telling him that a "personal" view is selfish and irresponsible. He seeks the "living world," the actual present and the actual past and not a conceptual present and conceptual past, and Solzhenitsyn is fully behind him. Unlike Rubin, Gleb has nothing to guide him except his own perceptions, his own experience, and a vague but insistent feeling that there *is* something called "spiritual wealth" (a lesson learned from the forced labor camps). He is willing to risk confusion and intellectual disorder. When Gleb indicts Stalin, one feels he has very little to go on. He is somewhat like the narrator of *The Gulag Archipelago*; the conventional resources and methods of scholarship and historiography are largely denied him, and he must rely on hunches, guesses, anecdotes, the word of friends and acquaintances, and the notion that one can assume the unseen larger and general truth if he can actually see smaller, local outcroppings of it. It all seems rather feeble and amateurish. It is like a jaunty little ant trying to burrow through a mountain range, picking his way as he goes. It is probably the only way.

Like Kostoglotov in *Cancer Ward* and Colonel Vorotýntsev in *August 1914*, Gleb Nerzhin in the middle of his life suddenly finds himself a seeker of truth, of the simplest truth. He is starting over, breaking out of the conceptual crust, moving carefully one step at a time toward a new faith or a decisive action that will free him from inherited systems of thought and government which sanction incompetency, cruelty, and murder. It is too bad that he must remain in prison. But one nearly forgets that grim fact in the light of his faith (which is Solzhenitsyn's) that even here a person *can* start over and rebuild his life. Abrupt dislocations are common in the Gulag world (often crushing, to be sure), and in his own life there Solzhenitsyn saw men who resolved to change themselves and then did so. Not many men, but a few. During this process the best men, like Gleb, keep alert for genuine wisdom and good advice (note Solzhenitsyn's interest in proverbs); people like the janitor Spiridon, untainted by post-revolutionary morality, assume new authority as wise men. But for the most part, as ideological accretions are being shucked off so that one can see things as they "are," a new trust is placed in oneself and in one's conscience and in the power and reality of the present moment—and for this reason many of Solzhenitsyn's heroes have a startling resemblance to that American tradition which gave us Anne Hutchinson, Emerson, Thoreau, Walt Whitman, and various other frontiersmen of the mind and spirit.

But most of the men in Mavrino, and some of those outside, discover that they are in hell, not on any spiritual frontier. "We must picture Hell," says C. S. Lewis,

> as a state where everyone is perpetually concerned about his own dignity and advancement, where everyone has a grievance, and where everyone lives the deadly serious passions of envy, self-importance, and resentment. . . .
> . . . I live in the Managerial Age, in a world of "Admin." The greatest evil is not now done in those sordid "dens of crime" that Dickens loved to paint. It is not done even in concentration camps and labour camps. In those we see its final result. But it is conceived and ordered (moved, seconded, carried, and minuted) in clean, carpeted, warmed, and well-lighted offices, by quiet men with white collars and cut fingernails and smooth-shaven cheeks who do not need to raise their voices. Hence, naturally enough, my symbol for Hell is something like the bureaucracy of a police state or the offices of a thoroughly nasty business concern.[12]

In *The First Circle*, as we move away from the sharashka and up into the offices of the bureaucracy, we do not always find quiet men who never raise their voices, but Lewis is right about *where* the greatest evil is done and, like Solzhenitsyn, he knows that individual men do it. Part of the ominous quality of *Ivan Denisovich* comes from the fact that both middle level administrators and those ultimately responsible for the prison are remote,

81

never seen. The reader can only guess about their assumptions and sensibilities, or not think of them at all, or take the view that the camp lives a life of its own in a forgotten corner of the earth and if the higher-ups only knew what went on, they would change things. In *Ivan Denisovich* there is no one to blame; in *The First Circle* we know exactly whom to blame. Perhaps we learn more than we want to about them. The higher the position of the men in charge, the more cruel, cunning, and vicious they are—and Solzhenitsyn sees to it that men like Oskolupov, Sevastoyanov, Abakumov, and Stalin are also pig-headed, silly, and mostly stupid.

Abakumov is a minister of state because he is a degree or two more cunning and distrustful than the men immediately below him and knows enough not to take them at their word. He is also capable of smashing people in the face, of exerting direct physical as well as psychological pressure on others—C. S. Lewis's view of the bosses as quiet-voiced men does not apply to the very highest level of Solzhenitsyn's world (although Stalin himself is most dangerous when he stops shouting). Violence often gets results. The temper tantrums of the Abakumovs are especially intimidating to those beneath them who are more sensitive and intelligent than they are and who themselves use memos rather than fists to conduct their violence. "Throughout his whole career he had lost out whenever he tried to think and he won when he acted out of zeal. So Abakumov burdened his mind as little as possible" (88).

But when something seems to be going wrong at the Mavrino Institute, Abakumov is at least bright enough to know how to find out the truth. A liar himself, he knows that Colonel Yakonov and Oskolupov, in order to appear efficient, will themselves lie and make promises they cannot keep, and so he goes directly to the source. He has engineers Pryanchikov and Bobynin taken from the sharashka in the middle of the night and brought to him. These men do the real work, know their business, and are indispensable members of the technological front line.

Abakumov's meetings with them, as is typical in *The First Circle* when a prisoner confronts an administrator, are occasions for Solzhenitsyn to test the prisoner (he knows, or thinks he knows, the administrator all too well). Pryanchikov fails the test. He gives Abakumov the information he is after, and he makes the minister pay no price for it. He is not a bad man; on the contrary, his friends notice his almost "unnatural sincerity" (90). His problem is that he is so deeply interested in his work that when Abakumov asks him about it he pours forth information like a faucet. He speaks to the minister as if they are both fellow lovers of science, but Abakumov only wants to know when the project will be completed. Abakumov does not care about the process or its scientific principles but about results (and results only because if he doesn't get them Stalin may have *him* shot). The Pryanchikovs of the world *can* be used by ruthless men. They love their research so much that they lose themselves in it or fail to see clearly its consequences. It is an appallingly simple and old story.

In fairness to Pryanchikov, however, it should be said that Abakumov takes him by surprise. Once out of Mavrino, on the drive to the Kremlin, Pryanchikov's "whole soul was stirred by the bright lights of Moscow, twinkling and glittering outside the windows of the Pobeda" (90); and shortly afterwards his attention is caught and held by the floor-length mirror in Abakumov's office: "For a zek who gets along with a cheap little mirror smaller than the palm of his hand and who doesn't always have that, it's a whole adventure to look at himself in a big mirror" (91). Pryanchikov is so enchanted with these rare delights that he begins answering Abakumov's questions without thinking, and only when the visit is over does he remember that he should complain about conditions in the sharashka.

Bobynin, on the other hand, gives Abakumov hell. Unlike Pryanchikov, he swaggers into the minister's office fully aware that this is an opportunity to deliver messages "to anyone at the top" (96). Chapter 17, devoted entirely to Bobynin's meeting with Abakumov, is the most succinct statement in the entire novel of how far out of touch the bureaucrats are with the aims and needs of the scientists themselves. Like a number of his fellow prisoners, Bobynin has had so much taken away from him already that he has nothing more to lose, and so he can speak frankly: A "person you've taken *everything* from," he tells Abakumov, "is no longer in your power. He's free all over again." This stoic attitude is voiced repeatedly in Solzhenitsyn's work, and one guesses that it was commonly heard among thoughtful prisoners of the author's acquaintance, but its force depends finally on who says it and under what circumstances. Abakumov doesn't seem much impressed. He doggedly insists on knowing when the project will be finished. Bobynin explodes and delivers a tirade which includes the bitter question, "Don't you suppose that in addition to giving orders you need calm, well-nourished, free people to do the work? And without all this atmosphere of suspicion" (97). At the conclusion of his speech Bobynin stands up "wrathful, big" (98); meanwhile, a "black rage" stings Abakumov's eyes. So Bobynin talks tough and makes Abakumov hurt a little for being Abakumov, and that is good. Still, despite Bobynin's moral victory here, the minister gets the information he needs, and Bobynin concludes, "I have to work tomorrow" (98). He protests the conditions, but he too will work. Because he is indispensable to the project, he knows he will not be shot or taken away for talking back to a minister of state. Earlier, Bobynin himself was an amused witness when a dispensable man, Khorobrov, sealed his fate with a far lesser form of insubordination.

I am not suggesting that Bobynin should make the ultimate sacrifice and refuse to work at all; Solzhenitsyn has other characters reach that terminus. But we should see that despite his admirable anger, Bobynin also helps keep the system afloat—and thus he is another answer to the question Solzhenitsyn continually asks in *The First Circle*: If the system is so bad, why do good men contribute to its survival? Some gifted men like Bobynin, who value pure science and cherish the pursuit of truth (within limits), want to work—indeed almost have to work—and if they do not work where they are, there is no other place. They make the best of it. At least Bobynin expresses his indignation clearly when he has the chance. That is better than nothing.

After we see how Abakumov operates, we move the final step up to Stalin himself (Chapters 18–21), and we find "only a little old man with a desiccated double chin," a figure so laughable as to be incredible. We see Stalin contemplating himself, wondering about his physical liabilities, remembering the past, trying to think, trying to write. Hans Björkegren has said that the

> view of Stalin as a distorter of ideology totally dominated fiction literature, memoirs and historical drama from the early sixties to the middle of that decade. The disclosure of this ideological "treason" was probably the most central theme of Solzhenitsyn's works in the sixties. This criticism is particularly painstaking in *The First Circle* and *Cancer Ward*. Almost everything else he has written demonstrates in different ways the tragic consequences of the Stalinist "treason" against the Leninist cause.[13]

According to Solzhenitsyn's portrait, it is true that Stalin's impenetrable egotism *does* cause him to think "how often he had warned and corrected the rash and too easily trusting Lenin" (101), but the main emphasis in these chapters is elsewhere. The author is seeking a special kind of revenge. It is not merely that he wishes to de-mythologize Stalin; he wishes to show him as a severely limited man who would be a pathetic clown had he not the capacity to do so much evil. Solzhenitsyn takes a risk when he presumes to read the mind of the historical Stalin, and it is fascinating to watch him imagine how Stalin would act in the privacy of his room late at night —but the author's anger is more interesting than his version of Stalin. Certainly Solzhenitsyn is in a better position than we are to guess the nature of the actual Stalin, and I know of no portrait of the dictator which is especially superior to this one. Anyone who has read *The White House Transcripts* of President Nixon and his associates realizes that in the inner sanctums of the most powerful people in the world the level of discourse can be abysmally low; nevertheless, the Stalin in *The First Circle* is most significant as a target for Solzhenitsyn's arrows rather than a fully credible character. The irony is too broad during these chapters, and line after line is delivered as if Solzhenitsyn had been storing them up for years: Stalin is a man with "fat fingers which left their traces on books" (99). "He was tormented by nausea" (100). Caviar "stuck to his teeth" (100). When he has difficulty thinking through a thesis, he asks himself, "Should he phone Beria?" (112). Whenever he appears at a public banquet, he places his hands on his stomach and smiles; the guests "thought the Omnipotent was smiling to favor them, but he was smiling because he was afraid" (113). He has a "brownish-gray, smallpox-pitted face" with a "great plow of a nose" (114). He "loved to listen to his old speeches at night" (120). He wrote "in the consciousness that his every word straightaway belonged to history" (120). "He had not trusted his mother" (122). "Just as King Midas turned everything to gold, Stalin turned everything to mediocrity" (123). He was growing "old like a dog" (134).

Bitterly amusing, yes, but the very excess of insights like these combined with more general explanations of Stalin's character and motivation makes it seem that Stalin is squatting in the palm of Solzhenitsyn's hand. Such a method rarely works with historical personages who, by the fact of having walked on the public stage, are subject to somewhat tentative interpretations of their private lives. Solzhenitsyn gives the impression of having illuminated so quickly and thoroughly every dark corner of Stalin's life that there is nothing left to say. The reader resists that closing off of possibilities. In *August 1914* he does the same with General Samsonov, but he takes longer to do it, and that makes a difference—though at times he goes too far with him as well.

Despite the weaknesses in the characterization of Stalin, however, the novel needs him, even if the world does not. It is important that the reader try to imagine along with Solzhenitsyn what kind of man he was. As Victor Erlich has said, the Stalin chapters, whatever "their shortcomings, represent an organic, perhaps an indispensable, element of the novel's structure not only because the picture of the system would not have been complete without its pivot, but, and more importantly, because Solzhenitsyn's conception of Stalin is an essential aspect of the moral dialectic which informs *The First Circle*." Erlich suggests among other things that Stalin's "free-floating paranoia" is a necessary contrast to the moral freedom of characters like Nerzhin and Khorobrov.[14]

Given Solzhenitsyn's consistent and wise habit of placing the blame ultimately on individuals rather than on systems, it is not surprising that he shows Stalin, limitations notwithstanding, as the man who pulls the strings of that system. From the citadel of his quarters, in the middle of the night, he makes policy decisions—"his best ideas" —which affect one-sixth of the world:

> the way to exchange old bonds for new ones to avoid paying the bondholders; what the sentences should be for absenteeism from work; how to stretch the working day and the work week; how to bind laborers and other employees permanently to their jobs; the edict concerning hard labor and the gallows; the dissolution of the Third International; the exile of traitor populations to Siberia (109).

At one point Solzhenitsyn has Stalin thinking that "he had everything nailed down for good, all motions stopped, all outlets plugged, all 200 million knew their place" (109) except for the collective farm youths. Nevertheless, Stalin feels frustrated. While in theory everything is set, in practice he knows there are problems:

> the slackened pace of construction, the delays in production, the output of low-quality goods, the bad planning,

87

the apathy toward the introduction of new technology and equipment, the refusal of young people to pioneer distant areas, the loss of grain in the fields, overexpenditure by bookkeepers, thievery at warehouses, swindling by managers, sabotage by prisoners, liberalism in the police, abuse of public housing, insolent speculators, greedy housewives, spoiled children, chatterboxes on streetcars, petty-minded "criticism" in literature, liberal tendencies in cinematography (103).

Total control, absolute management, eludes him. It is almost as if human beings do not want to be made perfect by Stalin. Solzhenitsyn then says of him:

All his life things had never worked out. They had neved worked out because there were always people who interfered. And when one had been removed, someone else always turned up to take his place (104).

In the hour-by-hour conduct of their lives people do not hasten to shape themselves to fit Stalin's plan. They cannot see their choices and lives reflected in his system, and his spies and planners cannot really reach the center of their lives. Stalin is frustrated because he is not God. He can always kill people, but he cannot make all of them live precisely as he wishes, despite his "iron will," his "inflexible will" (108). Like so many men of the people everywhere, he does not know much about people, and his ignorance in combination with his powerful office makes him the most dangerous man on the planet. The living world outside the Kremlin walls is not the same as the conceptual world within it. Force is the only way to bring the two in line, and even then the alignment is only partial and temporary. "Only he, Stalin, knew the path by which to lead humanity to happiness, how to shove its face into happiness like a blind puppy's into a bowl of milk—'There, drink up!' " (130)

Stalin's personal characteristics and his odd way of life are reflected in the entire bureaucratic structure which he controls. He is obsessed with security, he knows the value of fierce facial expressions, "mistrust" is his "world view"

(122), he does not really want things to be completely successful because no "one but himself must be able to do anything flawlessly" (123). We see petty Stalins everywhere in Solzhenitsyn's world, and it is strongly suggested in these chapters that if the man on top were a better man, simply a decent person, then everyone else would be better, too—even the Marxist-Leninist misapprehensions of human nature could be lived with.[15] To Solzhenitsyn, for a time, Khrushchev must have seemed that better man. It is reported in *The Gulag Archipelago* that among high-ranking Moscow officials only "in Khrushchev's home was the chauffeur seated at the family table instead of being put in the kitchen" (230).

Chapter 21, entitled "Old Age," takes a curious turn. Solzhenitsyn has Stalin imagining himself becoming "Emperor of the Planet" (130) when suddenly, as if nudged from on high, Stalin begins to wonder about God, his own religious upbringing, about the old pre-revolutionary days, about the words "Russia" and "homeland."

> In general Stalin noticed in himself a predisposition not only toward Orthodoxy but toward other elements and words associated with the old world—that world from which he had come and which, as a matter of duty, he had been destroying for forty years (132).

The chapter ends two pages later on a quite different note—Stalin is filled with "helpless terror"—but it is as if for a moment in his own commitment to an older world Solzhenitsyn himself cannot resist ascribing to his worst enemy some of his own longings. Are we meant to see that Stalin is trapped in his own malice, his own system? That he knows full well the hollowness of those assumptions on which the Soviet state rests? Or is he merely becoming soft-headed and frightened as he approaches death? Solzhenitsyn appears to want it both ways. It is remarkable how often in his fiction men who are living devils feel remorse or suddenly hear a little bell ringing from deep in their past which takes them back to a crossroads. That such monsters have tattered remnants of a conscience proves, in Solzhenitsyn's view at least, that conscience is as real as sunshine and cannot be denied—no matter how difficult conscience, like sunshine, may be to define.

In *Gulag Two*, in the chapter entitled "The Ascent," Solzhenitsyn makes his most important non-fictional statement to date on the effect of prison upon his own outlook: "It was granted me to carry away from my prison years on my bent back, which nearly broke beneath its load, this essential experience: *how* a human being becomes evil and *how* good" (615). If one had not read any other Solzhenitsyn, he might wonder at such a claim—so bald, so pretentious—but few other twentieth-century novelists have investigated as searchingly as he the processes by which some men turn themselves into monsters and how others manage to evolve into what he calls "human beings." Many people in his work are neither the one nor the other, but those in whom he is most interested, especially in *The First Circle* and *Cancer Ward*, are always moving toward evil or toward good, though let me hasten to add as he does that "even within hearts overwhelmed by evil, one small bridgehead of good is retained" and even in the best of hearts there is "an unuprooted small corner of evil" (615).

Simply asserted, this view is neither new nor compelling, but rendered in his fiction, with all its characterization and interplay of motives, its requisite situations, and its innumerable individual cases with countless variations, the concepts of good and evil come to life with astonishing authority and cease to be mere concepts. Solzhenitsyn is expert at giving convincing and specific instances where characters may choose good or evil, and where, if the choice is less than crystal clear, it is nevertheless clear enough for intelligent men to see if they truly wish to do so. Many readers will be inclined to regard moral choices as infinitely complex, shrouded in ambiguity, almost never clear-cut, perhaps irrelevant or even non-existent. "You see," says one American essayist on the subject of morality, "I want to be quite obstinate about insisting that we have no way of knowing—beyond that fundamental loyalty to the social code—what is 'right' and what is 'wrong,' what is 'good' and what 'evil.' "[16] Solzhenitsyn questions that attitude; he finds it innocent, bookish; it is as if he is saying, "Come on, now. We've all heard *that* a million times, but if you've lived in the real world at all, you know better." Once one develops a conscience, moral choices may be difficult but they are not unclear. The problem is developing, or uncovering, one's conscience, and then in honoring its dictates.

In *The First Circle*, more than in any of his other novels, Solzhenitsyn shows where the forks in the road lie for as many different types of people as he can. He is also interested in the *degree* to which a character is falling into corruption or is evolving into a human being—and this matter of degree is easy for us to overlook in a novel which moves in fits and starts, in which we are probably longing to be given something more like a conventional plot. So there are undoubtedly times when out of sheer impatience the reader, desiring more action, would just as soon forgo careful discriminations and label all the zeks good, all the sharashka officials bad, and all the free employees innocent—and leave it at that. But one of the best reasons for reading this novel more than once is to allow ourselves to become discriminating moralists for a change. *The First Circle* creates that role for us. Not many twentieth-century novels allow us such a luxury.

We are prepared to ask, then, how *does* a person become evil? Immediately following the Stalin chapters we learn about the past life of the Mavrino Institute's chief of operations, Anton Yakonov, a much more credible bad man than Solzhenitsyn's Stalin. Solzhenitsyn *knows* Yakonov, and so, as it turns out, do we. He seems almost American in his values. It was Colonel Yakonov who, seventy pages earlier, decided to send Nerzhin and Khorobrov "away," back to the labor camps and, likely, to their deaths. Like several men on the wrong side in *The*

First Circle (the wrong side is any occupation which supports the institution of the Gulag), Colonel Yakonov is sensitive, intelligent, and should know better. Although an MGB officer, he is a former zek himself, and therefore has been through an experience which could have saved his soul. In Chapter 22 he wanders late at night among the ruins of the Church of St. John the Baptist. As a result of the information received from Bobynin and Pryanchikov, minister Abakumov has just punched him in the nose and "raged like a mad beast" over the incompetence of the Mavrino Institute. Yakonov has known for a long time that when men are pushed by arbitrary time limits they can't do anything well and that Soviet life is infested with schedule-making, goal-setting bureaucrats who hinder real achievement. When "things were done this way," he thinks, "houses did not stand, bridges broke down, construction collapsed, harvests rotted or the seed did not come up at all" (138). Despite this knowledge, Yakonov has always tried to lose himself in some safe middle-level corner of the bureaucracy where he could "exercise over-all direction at a considerable remove" from the enterprise at hand and maintain his "reputation of being an expert without being responsible for anything" (51). Anyone familiar with American universities, corporations, unions, or governmental units knows his type. Now, however, Yakonov is in despair, fearful that everything is about to fall apart and that he will be sent "away" again himself. He has got himself in the spotlight and he can't escape; he is being held responsible for a project that in itself is irresponsible.

Why has he allowed himself to remain a Colonel of Engineers of the State Security Service for so long? He tells himself that he has "squirmed and struggled and played the dictator" (138) for the sake of his two small children and his beloved wife. At that, we may feel a twinge of sympathy; after all, Solzhenitsyn celebrates family love whenever he can. But it's not hard to love one's own family. Men who have nasty and immoral jobs often tell themselves the same thing, that all they are doing is facing reality in a harsh world, squirming and struggling for the sake of others, when all they really mean is their own family. That is a small achievement. There *is* some good in Yakonov ("one small bridgehead"), but not enough. His agony over his job is genuine but too recently acquired to have much stature; we know that he has worn "with dignity the silver shoulder boards with sky-blue edging" (51); he has enjoyed passing "the saluting guard at the gates wound with barbed wire" and slamming the door of his chauffeur-driven "personally assigned Pobeda car." Nevertheless, one may ask, aren't these forgivable vanities? We learn later (Chapter 73) that he also enjoys lounging in his pajamas in his rocking chair "among his many bookshelves" (528); his "droll little children" (527) already know how to speak English; his wife plays pleasant waltzes on the piano in their nicely furnished Moscow apartment. So where are we to find flaw or fault? He is not excessively greedy or ambitious. He just wants to be free to enjoy a few modest daily pleasures.

What is wrong is that the Yakanovs of the Soviet Union (and elsewhere) support institutions which they know sanction corruption, terror, and murder, but they cast this knowledge to the back of their minds. They want to preserve their little comforts; they like the trappings and the security of office; they love their families and are able to provide for them through the rewards the institution dispenses. Solzhenitsyn understands this administrative personality but does not forgive it. These are the very people who could, if they willed it and if they had the courage, change things. Yakonov could cause considerable trouble simply by laughing in Abakumov's face and refusing to obey his orders. The bureaucratic chain *could* be weakened. True, he and his family might lose everything, including their lives, but if only now and then a few Yakonovs would refuse to serve—then a few more, then dozens more, then hundreds—why maybe, just maybe, the whole foul system would begin to pull apart.

But that is not the way things work. Solzhenitsyn himself is our generation's expert on the lengths to which men regularly go in order to survive. He is our leading literary authority on the sheer value of life itself, of the need to keep breathing. In the *Gulag* books alone he gives hundreds of examples of men and mechanisms which prevent a counter-revolution from happening. Nevertheless, again and again, he returns to the question of why people do not resist. Despite his meticulous documentation of the complicated machinery which grinds men down and keeps heroic impulses in check, one recurrent note in all his works is a plea for just that—heroism. Under extraordinary peril, if a few cannot be heroic—larger than life— then institutions may grow which make peril commonplace for life on an ordinary scale. Early in *Gulag I,* in discussing the small victory of D. A. Rozhansky over Stalin, Solzhenitsyn remarks that "if people had been heroic in exercising their civil responsibilities, there would never have been any reason to write either this chapter or this book" (49). He has seen enough heroes in his lifetime to know that heroism is still possible. But the Yakonov mentality usually prevails in this world, and Solzhenitsyn also knows that every "man always has handy a dozen glib little reasons why he is right not to sacrifice himself" (*Gulag I,* 17). Yakonov has his own comfortable apartment and his own loving family; why should he care about other people? If part of his job is to send people away, then send them away he will.

He had at least two moments in his life when he might have taken a different turn, away from evil. In 1932, when he was a young radio engineer, he was arrested and then spent six years in prison, and ever since he has tried "to forget his prison past" (139) and steer clear of anyone who might remind him of that ignominious part of his life. Many former prisoners are like Yakonov; indeed, Solzhenitsyn often claims that "no one in our country can remember anything, for memory is the Russians' weak spot, especially memory of the bad" (*Gulag II,* 121). Yakonov's denial of his prison past means he learned nothing of value from it—and that is too bad. In Solzhenitsyn's terms he had the opportunity in prison to become a human being, to discover that he had a conscience and a soul, to "recognize genuine friendship" and to reap all the spiritual benefits that Solzhenitsyn enumerates in "The Ascent" chapter of *Gulag II*. But Yakonov was embarrassed by his imprisonment and now believes that

> the only people who go to prison are those who, at some moment in their lives, fail in intelligence. Really intelligent people look ahead; they may twist and dodge, but they always stay in one piece and in freedom (529).

Survival at any price is Yakonov's credo. And that is exactly what the majority of prisoners did learn. Prison was *not* a soul-saving experience for most of them; in fact, to survive at any price meant "at the price of someone else" (*Gulag II*, 603). And afterwards many of them found their nook and hunkered down in freedom and eventually became supporters of the very regime that put them away in the first place. As much as Solzhenitsyn believes in the possibility of heroic action and the spiritual value of suffering, he is the first to "admit the truth: At that great fork in the camp road, at that great divider of souls, it was not the majority of the prisoners that turned to the right" (*Gulag II*, 603).

In Yakonov's case it is implied that he did not make the right turn in prison because already, years earlier, he had made a more significant wrong turn, one that thousands of other young men and women made and continue to make. In Chapter 23 Yakonov is standing amidst the ruins of the old church—the Kremlin is in sight—and remembering a time twenty years before when a young girl, his fiancée Agniya, took him to this very spot, where they discussed religion and politics. Agniya was only twenty-one at the time, "slender and fragile" (142), uninterested in being up-to-date, an observer of the small beauties of the world, self-effacing, apprehensive of sex, "not born of this earth" (141), stubbornly on the side of all those who were being persecuted and arrested. She was not the kind of person Yakonov ought to have been interested in, and yet he was strangely attracted to her anyway. At twenty-six he was full of himself and knew all the Marxist-Leninist-Bolshevik certainties by heart; he loved to say things like, "One must recognize what is new in time, before it is too late, for whoever fails to do so will fall hopelessly behind" (148). Such a notion, especially when sanctioned by the state itself, can be almost irresistible to heedless young people. Yakonov wanted to be up-to-date and fashionable. Who can blame him? It is a powerful and compelling impulse, not unknown to Americans, either. But when keeping up becomes an article of faith (rather than a temporary sign of life) one finds oneself at the mercy of other people's visions of what is new and proper; it is not surprising that Yakonov spends the rest of his life squirming, adjusting, regretting. Throughout this scene at the old church we see that Agniya has an identity of her own and that Yakonov, like so many people who have answers for everything, does not. He has positions rather than beliefs, programs rather than values.

When Agniya ventures the opinion that the Church endured for so many centuries because "faith went deep" (146) and because orthodoxy was spiritually stronger than Islam, Yakonov condescendingly trots out the "real" reasons why the Church prevailed. Shy Agniya has no effective verbal reply; she is bewildered by Yakonov, and worried about him. She simply believes in an unseen world, and he on the other hand can explain everything under the sun—and that is one of the main reasons why he turns out to be such a thug later on. He stands there in the churchyard, flushed with the sheer excitement of his atheism. Agniya had brought him here, it seems, in hopes that its beauty and tradition would suggest that perhaps there *are* mysteries in this life, but the setting only feeds his ego. How strong he feels, a modern man in an outdated world! Monuments of superstition and ignorance stand all around him, no match for his own new knowledge.

In his youth Solzhenitsyn himself was an atheist, and

so he has a bit more sympathy for Yakonov than my discussion so far may suggest. Throughout Yakonov's conversation with Agniya, the reader gets the impression that Yakonov is listening to her with one ear open and could at any moment break down and take her point of view seriously. He likes her in spite of himself. Practically all the main characters in Solzhenitsyn's fiction have their "allotted" turning point, as it is called in *Gulag II* (624), and Yakonov is standing at his. Despite mouthing all those smug certainties, he is moved more than he wants to be by the church ceremonies. He does have a real choice before him. Agniya leads him inside the church (its window gratings are in "the ancient Russian style" [148]); she places a candle and Yakonov notices how "life and warmth" (148) are restored to her cheeks; when the litany is sung, for "the first time Yakonov understood the ecstasy and poetry of the prayer" and concludes that "no soulless church pedant had written that litany" (149). He is face-to-face with a dimension of experience which cannot be explained or dismissed as easily as he had thought. But he does not act on this realization. Shortly afterwards, for the sake of his advancement, he agrees to sign an article written by someone else which "was not the complete truth" (149). Agniya then rejects him, and he feels a "sense of relief"—which in reality is the beginning of the death of his conscience.

Solzhenitsyn wants us to understand, however, that a rejection of the "old" in favor of the "new," while always easy for thoughtless people, was especially easy to make at the time. Even Agniya's own mother and grandmother had rejected the Church because it had "accepted serfdom so easily" (145): To be a Bolshevik was to believe oneself on the very cutting edge of history, to be part of the making of a completely new social order, the pattern of the future—and this *was* one of those rare moments in human affairs when it was possible to believe this and not be a fool. But in 1949, as Yakonov sits in the ruined churchyard, his will to live gone, we are meant to see what he does not: The destruction of the Church and all it represents was a far more serious loss than the destruction of the Bolshevik dream. Yakonov looks out over the new Moscow and sees a skyscraper under construction (with a fence around it); by contrast, the church where he is sitting is described as "almost-wrecked" (150) and as having a "rusty door which had not been opened for many years" (149)—but that battered church could even now offer hope and comfort to Yakonov had his soul not dried up. The skyscraper offers nothing. As for the Bolshevik dream, Yakonov's own life is testimony to its failure. When he was young he told Agniya that the Bolsheviks

> believe no person should have arbitrary power over another person, they believe in the realm of reason. The main thing is they are for equality! Imagine it: universal, complete, absolute equality. No one will have privileges others don't have. No one will have an advantage either in income or in status (146).

But now all Yakonov can think about is the threatened loss of his high salary, his Moscow apartment, his Pobeda —and we have already seen him wield arbitrary power over people to defend his status and its benefits. Late in the novel we learn that the real motivating idea for most of his adult life had been that "people are all bastards" (528). Therefore, because everyone else is hopeless, one must look out for oneself and one's family.

Yakonov's early ardor on behalf of the Bolshevik dream of equality and his subsequent history of striving for something quite different is not unusual in Solzhenitsyn's world. Many of his characters have the same general biography. It is grimly amusing to see tucked into his narrative the countless small ways that most people, whether in prison or in freedom, deny equality, seek privileges, status, and more income. The Bolshevik dream has not come true and is not likely to. Apparently the only way to make it work is to lie about it and declare the kingdom of heaven at hand. Occasionally one may wonder if perhaps Solzhenitsyn is not suggesting that at least in some potential sense the Marxist-Leninist-Bolshevik view of man is valid and that if somehow we could have a purified form of it, life would be better. After all, some of Solzhenitsyn's most engaging characters believe this. But the answer is no. The materialistic view is dangerously incomplete, over-simplified, one-dimensional, and tempting. Most people who try to hold it for any length of time eventually become "spiritually disarmed," to use a phrase from *Gulag II* (626), easily corrupted. Although Solzhenitsyn would be the first to acknowledge the reality of evil within people, he would never, as Yakonov does, sum up human nature by declaring that people are all bastards. In Yakonov's case, his early dream, so appealingly shiny and clear-cut, helped to make his subsequent position inevitable. One sees in *The First Circle, Cancer Ward*, and several of Solzhenitsyn's short stories how cynical so many middle-aged Soviet men and women have become. After having lived for a generation with it, they do not really believe in the revolutionary ideology, but they have nothing to replace it with except money-grubbing and status-seeking. One finds almost as many fat Babbitts in Solzhenitsyn's Russia as in Sinclair Lewis's America.

Another outwardly comfortable but inwardly tormented official of the Mavrino Institute is Major Adam Roitman, Colonel Yakonov's deputy and rival. In Chapter 68 we find him lying awake in his Moscow apartment; his wife, "in a particularly graceful position" (487), is asleep at his side; his three-year-old son is in the next room. Although an MGB major and a Stalin Prize winner, he is also a Jew, and he is worried about a new outbreak of anti-Semitism initiated by Stalin himself. That does not seem fair to Roitman, especially because during "the Revolution, and for a long time afterward, the word 'Jew' had a connotation of greater reliability than the word 'Russian' " (489). Roitman is another middle-level bureaucrat who has always kept clear of trouble and "tried to do the right thing." He can understand why people might be persecuted because they are "members of a dominant caste, or hold certain political views or have certain acquaintances" (489), but for being a Jew? and a loyal Party member as well? In the course of the chapter Roitman suddenly remembers the time in his youth when as an ardent Young Pioneer he and his friends hatched a plot against the best student in their class, a thin, non-political lad named Oleg who believed that people have the right to say whatever they wanted to. Roitman and his friends persecuted Oleg unmercifully on the "grounds of anti-Semitism, attending church, and having an alien class origin" (493). Now, thirty years later, when he himself is under fire, the vileness of his participation in that event "made him flush with shame." He thinks, "A circle of wrongs, a circle of wrongs! And no way to break the vicious ring. No exit" (494).

Roitman's chagrin so long after the event is yet another example in *The First Circle* of a man on the wrong side acknowledging his errors and harkening for a moment to his conscience. His past comes back to haunt him—at least to an extent, at least enough to make him less than "happy." This happens so often in *The First Circle* that the reader may wonder if Solzhenitsyn isn't exaggerating or indulging in wishful thinking. Does he really believe that men eventually pay a price for their wickedness? that in hindsight they can see where they went wrong? that they become their own judges? For the intelligent ones, the answer seems to be yes. Solzhenitsyn attributes to Roitman an "inner self, his nighttime self" (489), which sees clearly and cannot be fooled, though it can certainly be ignored (Stalin, Yakonov, Rubin—all are given an equivalent faculty). Although there are many villains in Solzhenitsyn, few are contented. He probably *does* exaggerate the power of conscience, but that is because one of the purposes of the book is to demonstrate that such an entity exists in the first place.

For most of us, I would guess, no proof is necessary. We certainly don't believe that every man receives his just desserts, and neither does Solzhenitsyn: Stalin hardly receives his; the real-life Abakumov's imprisonment and execution seems too kind a fate for a man who imprisoned and executed millions; and virtually no Solzhenitsyn character in a powerful position undergoes a change of heart which then brings a dramatic change in his actions. But I doubt that very many people forever deceive themselves about their crimes. Those who sacrifice others to improve their own position, no matter how compelling their reasons (like Lev Rubin, Roitman, partly because he is a Jew, desperately "wants to belong" [489]), *do* seem to know what misery is and are quite frequently tortured by their own capacity for selfishness—even though they can live with it, too. It is unpleasant to be a selfish adult. Some readers are bound to be uneasy with Solzhenitsyn's presentation of conscience as fact rather than metaphor—it seems as old-fashioned as Hawthorne and Dickens—but in the daily non-literary lives of most of us, in terms of decisions actually made and of experiences actually remembered, we know exactly what Solzhenitsyn means. In their ordinary daily affairs people evaluate themselves according to starkly simpler standards than they might otherwise profess. Solzhenitsyn is aware of this fact. When a major failure occurs in a man's life, no matter how smart and sophisticated he is, he often wonders what he did to deserve it, and ends up tabulating his scorecard of good and bad deeds as if he had gone to church all his life and had never heard of moral relativism.

Adam Roitman has other problems, too. As in Bobynin's short chapter earlier, in which Bobynin articulates the grievances of all the scientists at Mavrino, Roitman's chapter is Solzhenitsyn's way of succinctly presenting a common managerial type, the man who "had slipped from being a creator into the role of boss of other creators" (490). As Roitman lies there next to his sleeping wife, he realizes that he has lost touch with his work; as a manager of others, "everything he was doing he was not doing himself" (490), and his life has lost its zest. Creativity—the "joy of a successful brain storm or the bitterness of unexpected defeat—had abandoned him" (491).

The moral of Roitman's story is that if you are lucky enough to have a job of useful work, stay with it. It is a treasure. At one time, Roitman had talent; most managers and administrators do not. What they do have is a genius for intrigue (in Roitman's case it is "the power struggle within the institute" [491]) and the minor virtue of being able to attend countless meetings and do mountains of soul-withering paperwork. Unlike those committed bureaucrats who love the intricacies of red tape, Roitman's tragedy is that he would prefer to "take the soldering iron in his own hand, sit in front of the green window of the oscilloscope and try to catch a particular curve, then he, like Pryanchikov, could hum a carefree boogie-woogie" (492–93). He wants to build something. He does not receive from his managerial work even the satisfaction of an Ivan Denisovich standing by his brick wall.

But we should not feel too sorry for Roitman. He has made mistakes, he would love to escape from the consequences of those mistakes, he is not happy, he has some good in him—yet he is not about to resign from his position. He may dream of being like Pryanchikov, but his dream is suspect. As we have seen, Pryanchikov is somewhat less than admirable. Men who lose themselves in the hills and dales of pure science, or who hope to find refuge in oscilloscopes, are easily used, as Roitman himself undoubtedly knows. It is too late for him. He will help keep the system going.

Prosecutor Makarygin has no regrets about his part in the system. He is the most successful of all the high officials we see in *The First Circle*, and the dinner party at his spacious apartment brings together fashionable Muscovites, most of whom are also successful in their respective fields and are comparatively secure and unworried. They are the cream of Soviet society. They are intelligent, charming, well-informed, or so they think, and they support the Stalinist regime because it has given them a good life. Although prosecutor Makarygin considers himself a revolutionary and a member of the working class, he and his family and friends could almost be having this party in a middle-class suburb of any capitalist city in the world. They value good food, nice clothes, fine furnishings, and high salaries; the prosecutor prefers detective stories to law books, and the pride and joy of his study is his collection of tobacco, pipes, and cigars. Part of Solzhenitsyn's purpose here is to draw an ironic parallel to Gleb Nerzhin's birthday party at the sharashka, where so much genuine feeling is shown by men who live such harsh lives. But the most important effect of the dinner party is to show the formidable complacence of the Makarygins and their circle. This class of people does not wish to change. Yakonov and Roitman spend half their time within the Gulag world and therefore know terror and intimidation at first hand; they too live outwardly successful lives, but they are also miserable ("No exit," Roitman thinks)—and if someone could lead them out of their misery they would follow him. But Makarygin and his friends are satisfied with their lot; their lives are full and interesting. They successfully manage their misery and distract their consciences. Much of the party talk concerns art, literature, and history; of course, Solzhenitsyn wants *us* to see that this talk is riddled with exaggeration and hypocrisy and overlaid with a veneer of truth-concealing jargon. Few among the group would be especially moved by the Gulag facts even if they were able, as we are, to read *The Gulag Archipelago*. "You live well, Makarygin," says "big-bellied" General Slovuta (422); and the jovial general is capable even of a grim witticism when he tells the prosecutor that he should marry his youngest daughter to a Chekist—"that's a solid investment" (423).

Several individuals at the party are meant to challenge this complacency: the soldier, Captain Shchagov; the old "die-hard" revolutionary, Radovich; the "pleasant-looking" young schoolmate of Clara Makarygin's who asks Alexei Lansky for help; and Clara herself. But the successful people are quite prepared for dissident views of the system they support. Although they do not want to hear about the Gulag world, they are not ignorant of its existence, either. They regard it as an unfortunate necessity or as an institution against which to measure their own achievements. The pleasant-looking schoolmate of Clara's asks Lansky to intervene on behalf of her dying father, a prisoner who has recently been paralyzed by a stroke; why, she asks, "must a person who is certain to die be kept in a camp?" Lansky replies:

> "If we reason that way, what is left of the law?" He smiled ironically. "After all, he was sentenced by a court. Can't you understand? And what does it mean anyway, 'to die in a camp'? People have to die—they die even in camps. People have to die somewhere. *When the time comes to die, does it make any difference where?"*
>
> He got up in annoyance and left.
>
> His words rang with that conviction and simplicity that leave even the cleverest orator powerless to retort (432).

The pleasant-looking girl immediately leaves the party. She had come only to speak to Lansky. But the young literary critic, an up-and-coming official at the Supreme Soviet, one of those destined to inherit a powerful position, has the language to resist her sort of appeal and the charm, intelligence, and cleverness to live a full life elsewhere (as his activities during the rest of the party suggest). He could just as easily use the reverse argument (we are a government of people rather than laws) if it suited him; he thinks himself an extraordinary person. Thirty years hence, in the manner of a Yakonov or a Roitman, he may remember this moment, but now all he is interested in is promoting his own career and having a good time.

It is possible to say that as long as individuals like the pleasant-looking girl keep hammering away at the complacent people, reminding them that they can be better than they are, then there is hope. If a few individuals continue to challenge the ready-made phrases, all is not lost. Prosecutor Makarygin gets horribly angry when his newly awakened daughter Clara mocks him for believing that his high salary represents "accumulated labor" and reminds him that he was a worker for only two years and a prosecutor for thirty (425–26), but in the end the prosecutor seems to regard her attack upon him more as the ingratitude of impetuous youth than as a devastating criticism of his life. He is worried about her opinion of him, but he is not going to change. The most he will do is make excuses for his prosperity.

When Makarygin's old friend Radovich *agrees* with Clara, we may begin to feel that the prosecutor is on the verge of a significant concession but, no, Radovich himself ends up sounding foolish, also locked into a lexicon that he has used too often before: "All I ask for," he says, "is Leninist purity!" (428). Radovich properly disapproves of the soft life of the Makarygins and sees that the prosecutor has betrayed the ideals of the Revolution, but his own moral authority is undermined by his quaint ideological orthodoxy: As everyone "in the Comintern predicted, I believe firmly that we will soon witness an armed conflict between America and England for world markets!" (429). This seems even sillier than the prosecutor's own clichés—and the prosecutor would rather smoke a cigar than discuss ideology anyway. As frequently happens in both *The First Circle* and *Cancer Ward*, characters argue themselves into amusingly extreme positions. At one point Radovich says, "Anyone who hasn't suffered in twenty years"—he means Makarygin, and he sounds like Solzhenitsyn himself—"shouldn't be allowed to dabble in philosophy." Makarygin replies, "You are a dried-up fanatic! A mummy! A prehistoric Communist!" (428). Both men do make some sense, but a perspective-giving humor is also part of this scene. Characteristically, as earnest and didactic as he is himself, Solzhenitsyn wants us to know how ridiculous didactic and earnest voices can sound.

Radovich, Clara, and the pleasant-looking girl are no threat to the party-goers. They seem like cranks and are easily dismissed. It is nice that a few dissenters do exist outside prison, but *The First Circle* also shows why they have had so little influence.

But is that conclusion valid? What about those people in the novel who resist injustice and are willing to make heroic sacrifices? Isn't Solzhenitsyn above all a hopeful writer? Isn't his ability to convince us of the reality and effectiveness of heroic action among the things setting him apart from most modern writers? Or are we to assume that the sacrifices of Gleb Nerzhin, Innokenty Volodin, and the resistance of people like Clara and her friend are merely isolated acts which do not necessarily have positive implications for the future? Most of the decent people in *The First Circle* land in prison. We are told more than once how a "whole generation had been taught to believe that 'pity' was a shameful feeling, that 'goodness' was to be laughed at, that 'conscience' was priestly jargon" (300). One of Nadya Nerzhin's roommates, Olenka, dismisses love as merely "a transcendental idea" (316). Nadya herself is worried about her husband's use of the word God—"Prison was crippling his spirit," she thinks, "leading him off into idealism, mysticism, teaching him submissiveness" (318). On the one hand, Solzhenitsyn has strong opinions about the miseducation of the younger generation (which in both *The First Circle* and *Cancer Ward* includes people from seventeen to about thirty-five), but on the other hand, much of his energy goes into portraying individual exceptions to that pleasure-seeking, thoughtless, glib, strictly materialistic generation. Innokenty Volodin is, after all, prosecutor Makarygin's son-in-law and about as fashionably modern as they come, but he eventually finds himself capable of sacrificing everything for the sake of truth and conscience. As we have seen, there are others like him, though not many.

So the "hope" is invested in a comparatively few individuals, not in a rising new generation of dissenters. Few young people will undergo the transformation of an Innokenty because few know how to think. (Of course, there is always that underlying, hoping-against-hope whis-

106

per in Solzhenitsyn's work: If only more people *would* think.) In prison, where suffering and deprivation are the rule, such transformations, though not common, are more likely to occur, but for people like Innokenty and Clara to be transformed is rare indeed. The hope is not that some group will emerge to save the country from itself— that has happened before—but that more individuals will become "human beings," a flat and insipid phrase, it may seem, but Solzhenitsyn trusts us to know what it means. The very structures of *The First Circle* and *Cancer Ward* show the interplay of individual cases; the reader is continually in the position of looking for a few good human beings. And now and then one of them *does* have an influence. The arrest of Innokenty will, we are told, ruin his father-in-law's career—"this would be a blotch on his record" (631)—and so in the end the Makarygin complacency *is* violated because of a son-in-law's conscience. One is reminded of the Russian proverb Solzhenitsyn uses in his Nobel Prize Lecture: "One word of truth shall outweigh the whole world." We would all like to believe so.

At first, the married life of Innokenty and Dotnara (Makarygin) Volodin is happy as can be. "We have only one life" (394) is their philosophy; if one is able—and the Volodins are—one should live it to the hilt. They travel throughout Europe, they attend "an act or two of every unusual play" (394), they dance, sail, play tennis, avoid having children. Even though he doesn't know quite what the word means, Innokenty is proud to be known as an epicurean; the Volodins "tried every new and strange fruit" (394). The best years of their life occur while the world is at war, but "none of the world's grief touched Innokenty and Dotnara" (394). After the war, however, after six years of living as most young people would like to, Innokenty becomes dissatisfied with himself and his friends—and the reasons given are not unfamiliar to American readers, most of whom are well aware of the limitations of "the chic life," as Solzhenitsyn calls it, even though they may be trying to live it themselves.

By now it is obvious that Solzhenitsyn regards a direct

and single-minded pursuit of pleasure as the surest way to misery. American readers may become impatient with this stance not because they fear its truth but because Solzhenitsyn so often seems to make it a matter of revelation and gives so many, many examples of different people learning that lesson. Some of us are likely to believe that we know better than he about self-indulgent pleasure-seekers—and maybe we do, since the possibilities for pleasure seem so much greater in the United States. But it is also true that no systematic government-sponsored effort has been made here to force everyone to accept a single ideology which depends for its glamor more on rejecting "old-fashioned" values than on providing clear new ones. Solzhenitsyn is trying to restore meaning to old-fashioned words, words that have been under attack throughout this century, and he is trying to demonstrate that self-sacrifice is better than self-indulgence. That is difficult to do. One reason for his prolixity is that he must make this case over and over again; he knows he is working against the grain of our biases.

Innokenty decides one day to learn the proper meaning of "epicurean" and while poking about among his dead mother's dusty old bookshelves (themselves emitting a "breeze of renewal" [395]) he finds her letters and diaries. Not only does he discover that she was a person, but he learns that she was in love with another man and not his father. As any son would be, he is shocked, surprised, interested. For the first time in his life, Innokenty finds himself moving outside of himself, taking seriously a person he had previously taken for granted. He immerses himself in his mother's words. Even though she says things which were "simply not correct" (397), he keeps on reading:

> The very words in which his mother and her women friends had expressed themselves were old-fashioned. They wrote, in dead seriousness, with capital letters: "Truth, Beauty, Good, Evil: ethical imperatives." In the language Innokenty and his friends used, words were

more concrete, and therefore more comprehensible: moral intelligence, humaneness, loyalty, purposefulness (398).

His mother used the old-fashioned words, but she also lived a full, free, intellectual life of her own; her diaries and letters are packed with references to artists, writers, magazines, and cultural events which Innokenty has never heard of and of which there is officially no trace. It dawns on him how shallow are his and his wife's lives by comparison, how much they are prisoners of their narrow values and limited education. He reteaches himself how to read, and he reads "erroneous" and "outcast" books, whereas before he read "only the clearly established classics" (399). He begins to think.

Clara Makarygin eventually does the same. It is that simple. On every page of *The Gulag Archipelago* we sense a narrator who is thinking for himself, as if awakening after a long sleep and trying to sort out a vastly more confusing world than he ever knew existed. In any society, but especially in a highly-planned bureaucracy, thinking for oneself is not as easy as it sounds. The great promise of Soviet socialism is security for all members of society —the bottom will not drop out, no one will suddenly go broke or be without a "place"—and in exchange for that security people tacitly accept, as Innokenty Volodin did for most of his life, that there is only one way to view the world. Everyone wants to be secure, and if like the young Innokenty one has not only security but mobility and all the comforts of "the chic life," there is no compelling reason to think for oneself. One needs to be shocked into it—by prison, perhaps, or by the sort of discovery Innokenty makes, or by working closely with "enemies" of the state as Clara Makarygin does. Innokenty and Clara are two people in freedom who appear to have everything; but they are thrust mentally outside the pre-established forms of Soviet society and finally reach the same conclusions about that society as its declared enemies, people like Gleb Nerzhin.

109

Chapter 84, entitled "Second Wind," is among the most significant in the novel because it shows the full extent of Innokenty's transformation. Solzhenitsyn must convince us that a person who has known a lush and pleasurable life *can* undergo such a dramatic change of values —and not merely because that person wishes to make a virtue of necessity now that he has been arrested and imprisoned. Innokenty is continuing to think:

> Suddenly it was as though a film had been removed from his brain, and what he had read and thought about during the office that day emerged with full clarity:
> "Faith in immortality was born of the greed of unsatisfied people. . . . The wise man finds his life span sufficient to complete the full circle of attainable pleasures. . . ."
> But was it really a matter of pleasures? He had had money, good clothes, esteem, women, wine, travel, but at this moment he would have hurled all those pleasures into the nether world for justice and truth . . . and nothing more (360).

Do justice and truth matter more than pleasure? Most people don't think so. And even in this passage one wonders whether if Innokenty loved his wife (he does not) he would trade *her* for justice and truth—money, good clothes, and wine, yes, those *are* tradable commodities. Elsewhere in Solzhenitsyn we see how much small pleasures matter to men in prison, how at times a man is willing to trade almost anything for a cigarette or an extra helping of gruel. But of course the point Solzhenitsyn wishes to make is that thoughtful men are not pleasure-seekers, though they know how to appreciate a pleasure when it comes their way ("With a shudder of happiness Innokenty drank the second cup, without sugar but sensing sharply the aroma of the tea" [643]). By the end of the chapter the former epicurean has rejected epicureanism entirely ("the wisdom of the ancient philosopher seemed like the babbling of a child" [643]). He has re-

110

turned to the old-fashioned words. He sounds like his mother.

Probably the only thing a person needs to know in this world is the difference between good and evil. How does he learn the difference? It helps to suffer or to pass through harrowing experiences. If you have eyes to see and a heart to feel, you will discover that those fundamental questions which once seemed ambiguous (e.g., does evil exist? what is its nature?) have ceased to be matters of airy speculation. Experience, hard experience, will teach you this—if you are as smart as you think you are. Good and evil are abstractions only to innocent people. In prison, a glass of water or a piece of thread or a button is good; a fist or a bright light in your face is evil —and so with the person who gives you the one or the other.

But the Solzhenitsyn we are discussing here is a novelist, not a philosopher. His "proof" of the above is not made according to the laws of logic. He wants us to feel the reality of Innokenty's transformation by having us share intimately, step by step, what happens to him from the moment of his arrest to his concluding sentiments (Chapters 82 to 84). He gives us every little stitch of fact and Innokenty's reactions. That is all he can do as a novelist. He wants us to see that good and evil are being defined by Innokenty with each movement of his mind. Those forty pages are among the best writing in Solzhenitsyn's work—undoubtedly a vivid memory from his own experience. They map out the entrance to hell. And there is a curious sort of challenge to them. Just as the prisoners in Solzhenitsyn often present credentials to one another proving that they have been through a harrowing enough experience to make them worth listening to, here the reader is asked by implication to present his credentials for disbelieving Innokenty's transformation. The suggestion is that only people who have never been here could possibly believe in silly assertions like Epicurus's "Inner feelings of satisfaction and dissatisfaction are the highest criteria of good and evil" (643).

111

"Simplicity, simplicity, simplicity!" says Thoreau:

> I say, let your affairs be as two or three, and not a hundred or a thousand; instead of a million count half a dozen, and keep your accounts on your thumb nail. In the midst of this chopping sea of civilized life, such are the clouds and storms and quicksands and thousand and one items to be allowed for, that a man has to live, if he would not founder and go to the bottom and not make his port at all, by dead reckoning, and he must be a great calculator indeed who succeeds. Simplify, simplify.

All of Solzhenitsyn's heroes, to one degree or another, eventually simplify—usually at first by force and then by choice. As Thoreau would put it, they learn to live "deliberately." Innokenty has been "lifted" to "heights of struggling and suffering" (643) which allow him to come to a few simple conclusions about life. Although Solzhenitsyn puts more stock than Thoreau in the regenerative power of physical suffering, both writers often sound remarkably alike in their notion of what constitutes true wisdom and how to achieve it. It almost always involves renunciation and self-discipline. "Most of the luxuries, and many of the so called comforts of life," says Thoreau —and this could easily be Solzhenitsyn describing Innokenty or Kostoglotov in *Cancer Ward*—"are not only not indispensable, but positive hindrances to the elevation of mankind."

And both writers can be accused of arriving at conclusions which, when set against the complexities of modern life, seem not sturdily simple at all, but simple-minded. Recently a popular magazine said of Solzhenitsyn that "as a prophet he has a vision so simple, single-minded and absolute that it cannot cope with a real and complex world."[17] The reference was not to his fiction but to one of his public pronouncements about international politics, and yet careless readers could (and do) say the same about his fiction, largely because his heroes, by the end of their stories, *do* know what they believe and somewhere along the line they have acted on those beliefs. Yes, their beliefs are simple (or evolving toward simplicity), but it is an earned and considered simplicity (quite unlike inherited ideology), and it is not earned in a vacuum. Solzhenitsyn knows as well as anyone about the "real and complex" world and is well-versed not only in prison-camp lore but in the tenets of modernism. If his heroes do seem simple, single-minded, and absolute (old-fashioned?), it is not because they are oblivious to the complexities of the modern world.

Consider Gleb Nerzhin. As we saw earlier, he enters the novel as a veteran prisoner who is already skeptical of Marxist dogma, already tough-minded ("We live—that's the meaning" of life [38]), already an individualist, and already capable of a decisive action based on principle. After all, in Chapter 9 of an eighty-seven-chapter novel he makes the decision which he knows will keep him in prison camps indefinitely. He sets a standard for heroism which few others can match (except for Gerasimovich's absolutely clear-cut: "I don't set traps for human beings!" [583]). And yet it is also fair to say that he does not know, or does not yet realize, what he believes. At this point in the novel much of what he says and does is based on instinct and intuition, faculties which he has yet to acknowledge as having authority. His friend, label-loving Lev Rubin, is partly right to call him an "eclectic" who plucks "bright feathers from everywhere" (39)—and, as Varsonofiev in *August 1914* says, eclecticism "is always easier—anyone can play at it" (467). The reason Gleb's role in the novel doesn't end in Chapter 9 is that Solzhenitsyn wants him to make further discoveries about "life," even though we, as modernist readers, might be perfectly satisfied with Gleb as he is: an intelligent but skeptical modern man who can recognize nonsense when he sees it. To suit us, he doesn't *have* to have a positive set of beliefs. But Solzhenitsyn takes Gleb beyond that position. As John B. Dunlop puts it:

. . . some critics have chosen to see Solzhenitsyn as a

preacher of enlightened skepticism. Such critics have
missed the extreme dissatisfaction with skepticism which
Nerzhin manifests in the course of the novel. . . . *The
First Circle* presents us with the *odyssey of a skeptic*. In
his dealings with his fellow zeks Nerzhin tests out his
new-found philosophy of skepticism and finds it
lacking.[18]

During the three days which constitute the action of the
novel, Gleb has significant discussions with a number of
people, in addition to Lev Rubin, who inadvertently help
him to develop an even newer attitude of mind. In the
end, according to Dunlop, he has a dual personality, "half
man-of-action and half mystic-contemplative" (*Dunlop*,
254).

One of those with whom he has discussions is Ruska
Doronin, who admires Gleb and listens to him in much
the same way that Gleb himself admires and listens to
Dmitri Sologdin. Ruska, early in the novel, has adopted
Gleb's skepticism: "All history is one continuous pesti-
lence. There is no truth and no illusion. There is nowhere
to appeal and nowhere to go" (78). But Gleb balks when
he hears Ruska talk like this. A strong young man living
among prison camp intellectuals and confused by so
many conflicting points of view can say and believe that
for a time, and Gleb is the first to admit that skepticism is
necessary "to split the rockheads" (78), but now he is
also wondering if one doesn't after all need "firm ground"
(78) to stand on and whether it isn't "also necessary to
love something" (79). Hearing his own views come so
confidently back at him forces Gleb to see how limited
they are, how pat and presumptuous they sound. His and
Ruska's conversation quickly returns to earth, as philosophical conversations often do in Solzhenitsyn, when
Ruska agrees that it is necessary to love something, "not
history and not theory, but a woman!" (79) Gleb is then
reminded that he himself has a rendezvous the day after
tomorrow in the acoustics lab with Simochka—and he
can hardly wait. (Tomorrow, however, Gleb will have an
unexpected visit with his wife, and in honor of that visit

will choose not to indulge himself with the willing, pathetic, and somewhat unreal Simochka.)

Another person with whom Gleb has discussions is Dmitri Sologdin. Sologdin appears to be the most admirable man in the sharashka, and it is not surprising that Gleb has found himself influenced by him. Sologdin already has spent twelve years in various camps; he has never seen his own son; he has suffered:

> There had been sleeplessness, exhaustion, and loss of body fluids. Long ago his name and his future had been trampled into the mud. His personal property was a used pair of padded cotton pants, now kept in the prisoners' check room in expectation of worse times ahead. . . . He could breathe fresh air only at certain fixed hours permitted by the prison administration (151).

Despite all this, there is "peace in his soul" and his "eyes shone like those of a youth" (151). He has already taught Gleb the valuable lesson that "a person shouldn't regard prison solely as a curse but also as a blessing" (158). He believes that prison is the best place to "understand the role of good and evil in human life" (157), and he is interested in self-culture, and he has an Emerson-like fondness for inspirational nuggets:

> Books and other people's opinions are shears which sever the life of a thought. One must first come upon the thought oneself. Later on one can verify it in a book (159).[19]

Sologdin's self-reliance forces him into eccentric postures (his private "language of maximum clarity," his perversely nonsensical opinions on all sorts of subjects as a means of combatting boredom, his wood-cutting), but it also allows him to design on his own the "absolute encoder," which all the other engineers working together had failed to do. Working alone, free from pressure, following his own intuitions, he proves his point "that great ideas are born only in a single mind" (199). Like Ivan Denisovich or Colonel Vorotýntsev in *August 1914,* he can work wonders when left to his own devices; by comparison to this one man, the communal groups within the sharashka are ineffective.

But something is wrong with Sologdin, too. Even with his brilliant mind, sparkling personality, and impeccable credentials as an experienced sufferer, he has "associated only with educated people" (154) during all these years, avoiding the uncultured like the plague. Gleb eventually realizes that a significant dimension of experience is lost to a man who actually believes, as Sologdin does, that only "unique personalities, shining and separate, like singing stars strewn through the dark heaven of existence, carry within them supreme understanding" (449). Sologdin's individualism goes too far, and in the end, just when we begin to think that he may indeed choose not to capitalize on the power his new design has given him, he decides to save himself by going along with the Institute's project. Most people would do the same, especially if they had already given twelve years of their lives to Gulag, but judged by the rigorous standards of *The First Circle* that decision is wrong. Sologdin cares too much about himself. It is as if he is enamored of his own genius and thinks he has the *right* to be self-centered. Despite his talk about spirituality and good and evil, Sologdin lacks the moral decisiveness which Gleb finds in the peasant Spiridon, a person Sologdin does not take seriously. And Sologdin, thinking himself to be defending morality, also has an argument with Lev Rubin which becomes personal and vicious. Other people matter less to him than the constructions of his own energetic mind.

Long before the end, we should see that Sologdin, despite his talents, is a little too sure of himself, too confident of his own self-discipline and will-power—which is undermined soon enough, to be sure, when the sexy Ermina seduces him in an implausible and silly scene—and too much the pontificating guru: "You have matured greatly," he tells Gleb at one point (159). The "rules" he gives Gleb are not stupid, but they are invariably exaggerations of positions which are elsewhere sponsored

116

by the best men in Solzhenitsyn's world ("But when difficulties arise out of increasing objective resistance," says Sologdin, "that's *marvelous!*" [160]). Moreover, they seemed canned and memorized, as if Sologdin were as much interested in conceiving them and working them into artful aphorisms as in their practical application. I may be wrong, though. Recently I attended a dinner where a football coach quoted Sologdin's famous "rule of the final inch" and claimed it was the inspiration behind his team's winning the league championship—and I believed the coach and I believe Sologdin. Not to shirk the last "crucial work" is important in any endeavor, but coming from Sologdin the emphasis on "the attainment of perfection" (161) is overblown, a kind of intellectual braggadocio on his part, a sign that he lacks the humility of a Gleb Nerzhin. Solzhenitsyn values self-reliance, but he also realizes that it can become as dogmatic in its way as Marxism.

At the very end, just before Gleb is taken away in the meat wagon, Sologdin offers him the chance to stay on at Mavrino. Gleb replies:

> "Thank you, Dmitri. I had that chance. But for some reason I'm in a mood to try an experiment for myself. The proverb says: 'It's not the sea that drowns you, it's the puddle.' I want to try launching myself into the sea" (658).

The tone of that reply defines the difference between the two men. Gleb is calm, undogmatic; his future is uncertain, but he knows his decision was right and not merely an impulsive anti-authoritarian gesture. He has more to learn; he is not ready, like Sologdin, to issue "rules of thought and life" (658); but he *has* acknowledged the reality of good and evil, the force of conscience, and after his renunciation of Simochka "he was happy he had acted as he had. He was moved . . . as if it were someone else who had made the great decision" (603). He has changed.[20] He is no longer a skeptic. A few simple truths are emerging for him.

117

But the change in Gleb is not announced as loudly as the change in Innokenty, who has only recently learned to think for himself, whose new perceptions come with lightning-like force. Gleb enters the novel as a thinker, and he has spent much more time than Innokenty among intellectuals. It would be implausible if he became an overnight convert to, say, Christianity. He has long ago rejected the pedestrian Marxist dogma that existence determines consciousness, but when Nadya accuses him of believing in God he won't quite admit that he does (he would be embarrassed). Although he is intrigued, he does not clap hands and shout "That's it!" when exposed to the extreme idealism of Kondrashev-Ivanov. He envies and will never dismiss the solid certainties of Spiridon ("Not one of the eternal questions about the validity of our sensory perceptions and the inadequacy of our knowledge of our inner lives tormented Spiridon. He knew unshakably what he saw, heard, smelled, and understood" [460]), but he cannot *be* a Spiridon, either. He doesn't leave the novel with all his questions answered, and at no point does he say, "I am becoming an idealist, with one eye on the unseen world and the other on the ground beneath my feet," but that is where he is heading. That such men still exist in Solzhenitsyn's world is its hope.

As the van takes Gleb and the others away, they fall silent:

> Yes, the taiga and the tundra awaited them, the record cold of Oymyakon and the copper excavations of Dzhezkazgan; pick and barrow; starvation rations of soggy bread; the hospital; death. The very worst.
> But there was peace in their hearts.
> They were filled with the fearlessness of those who have lost *everything*, the fearlessness which is not easy to come by but which endures (673).

The very last word of the novel is given to a Western journalist who fails to see the significance of the meat wagon—"the gay orange and blue van"—and by extension the entire story. Let us hope that is no longer true.

118

CHAPTER THREE

Cancer Ward

Solzhenitsyn began writing *The First Circle* in 1955 but did not complete it until 1964. Meanwhile, in 1963, he began *Cancer Ward*. Although he himself has said little about matters of craft, clearly in this, his second long novel, Solzhenitsyn learned to keep better control of his material. *Cancer Ward* is firmly organized, and the polyphonic technique is used here without caprice. The characters, issues, and conflicts are introduced and developed with a sense of timing on Solzhenitsyn's part that allows the novel to unfold smoothly, without nearly as many of those fragments, false starts, and dead ends which in *The First Circle* are so distracting. *Cancer Ward* has its implausibilities, exaggerations, and oddities, often having to do with male-female relationships, but one never feels that entire chapters should be deleted. The larger units fit together neatly.

Even though several are literally dying, the principal

119

characters are more consistently lifelike than their counter-
parts in *The First Circle*. This is partly because they are
given more space upon their initial appearance and therefore we know them better from the start: Rusanov, for
instance, is given the entire first two chapters. And, compared to those in *The First Circle*, the problems faced by
the characters have a different quality to them and probably are potentially more universal. The patients suffer
from immediate, graphically described physical pain as
well as the pressing anxieties associated with imminent
surgery, amputations, and death; the personality clashes as
well as the alliances and friendships have a time-is-run-
ning-out urgency to them; because of the large role of
women in the novel, possibilities for commonplace but
interesting complications are always present; and rather
than cream-of-the-crop engineers and scientists, most of
the patients are ordinary people who discuss basic issues
with plain talk and often blunt humor.

Cancer Ward is also invigorated by the fact that its
main character, Oleg Kostoglotov, after a long period of
imprisonment, exile, and sickness, is gradually returning
to life and slowly tasting (some of) its delights; along
with all the grayness and all the pain, there is joy and
celebration in this novel. Because the hospital is not a
prison, the world of *Cancer Ward* seems rounder, fuller,
indeed a little freer, than the worlds of the two previous
novels. Many of its characters continue to rebel against
the system; many are deeply concerned with the moral
and spiritual aridity around them; many of them *are*, to
borrow Max Weber's phrase, caught in the "iron cage" of
the bureaucracy,[1] and Moscow *does* cast its shadow over
the hospital (Rusanov monitors the news from the capital
as carefully as he does his own tumor). But that scream-
ingly outraged tone which Solzhenitsyn uses elsewhere is
generally absent from *Cancer Ward*. The voice of protest,
though still present, is quieter, as if Solzhenitsyn knows
that by now its existence can be taken for granted by his
readers.

All the action of *Cancer Ward* takes place in 1955 in

or around the cancer clinic at Tashkent, Uzbek S.S.R., where Solzhenitsyn himself was a patient early in 1954. The first two chapters introduce Pavel Nikolayevich Rusanov, a Party member and middle-level administrator who has developed an enormous tumor on his neck. He has come to the clinic to be cured. His self-important manner and superior attitude are hateful, and the reader is bound to wonder if the cancer that threatens his "whole happy life, so well thought out, so harmonious and useful"[2] will change him, make him into a better person before he dies. Rusanov will be one of the central characters in the novel.

In Chapter 3, we meet Zoya, a pretty, sexually experienced nurse, who for a short time will be romantically interested in Oleg Kostoglotov, and we meet Kostoglotov himself, lively and alert, recovering rapidly from his own illness, almost ready to be discharged. He is a former prisoner in a forced labor camp who after only a short time in exile (in Kazakhstan, in perpetuity) came to this clinic; once discharged, he will return to his exile in the tiny village of Ush-Terek. Kostoglotov is the main character in *Cancer Ward*, and like Gleb Nerzhin's his life bears some resemblance to Solzhenitsyn's own. Also in Chapter 3 we meet Nellya, a work-resenting orderly, and the young Tartar, Sibgatov, who "after three years of continuous, oppressive illness" is nevertheless "the gentlest and most courteous patient in the whole clinic" (26).

Chapters 4 and 5 are devoted mostly to the problems of the cancer ward as seen from the point of view of two doctors: Vera Gangart and Ludmila Dontsova, the head of the radiotherapy department. As the doctors make their rounds, other characters are introduced and the various doctor-patient relationships begin to take shape. We discover that Vera Gangart and Kostoglotov are attracted to each other. Ludmila Dontsova, suffering from radiation sickness herself, has a long conversation with Kostoglotov about the ethics of radiotherapy and the hospital's right to treat patients against their will or without fully knowing the consequences of that treatment. We see how the overworked Dontsova skillfully handles her anxieties, her professional commitments, and her private life.

Chapter 8 introduces Yefrem Podduyev, a fifty-year-old construction worker, who just before he dies finds himself interested in the question, what do men live by, which also becomes the principal question of the novel. We meet Yevgenia Ustinovna, the senior surgeon, who has spent her life cutting out cancers and who examines the patients from a different perspective than the radiotherapists, Gangart and Dontsova. She decides to release the tractor driver Proshka, who gleefully clutches his discharge certificates, on one of which is written: "*Tumor cordis, casus inoperabilis*" (115). After Proshka's story, we go to sixteen-year-old Dyomka, whose life has been difficult, who has "never had enough to eat" (122), yet who is cheerful, a truth-seeker, and wants to find people to talk to. Among others he finds old-fashioned Aunt Styofa, who believes that he should submit to God, and he finds new-fashioned Asya, who believes that life "is for happiness" (128).

Chapter 11 tells us more about Kostoglotov. He introduces into the ward the possibility of its acquiring an old Russian folk cure for cancer—a birch tree fungus. As dubious a cure as it seems, everyone listens to him. Then we switch to Zoya's point of view. She is interested in sex and marriage, in finding a good man, even in the possibility of joining Kostoglotov in exile after his discharge. And Oleg is delighted that such a beautiful young woman is willing to take a step in his direction. We move next to Rusanov and two chapters about his fears, family, job, and values.

Dyomka has a conversation with Vadim, a young geologist and patriot who appears to have the answers to a number of Dyomka's questions. We learn more about Yefrem Podduyev's past and witness some of the final realizations of his life. Rusanov has a nightmare. Vera Gangart and Oleg have a talk about a potentially dangerous root from Issyk Kul (Kostoglotov has reservations about the efficacy of modern medical science), which can kill pain but also people. It becomes clear that Vera is falling in love with Oleg. For a time he believes she is married, but we know she is a virgin whose would-be lover died in the war. To complicate matters, even though Oleg seems to want to return her love, he lusts after Zoya, who is more receptive to his immediate needs. Another feature of the Oleg-Vera-Zoya triangle is that the life-saving injections Vera has prescribed for Oleg are also slowly rendering him impotent. Zoya informs him of that unfortunate fact and also agrees to stop giving him the injections.

Meanwhile, Yefrem Podduyev is released from the ward, dies almost immediately at the railroad station, and we see how various people respond to that news. We see the difference between Vadim and Rusanov, both of whom are committed Communists. We learn about Kostoglotov's life in exile at his "lovely Ush-Terek" (259) and about his friends the Kadmins, a fine old couple who were "happy with what they had" (272). Aviette, Rusanov's fashionable daughter, pays a visit, and the values of yet another member of the younger generation are revealed.

Part II opens with a letter from Kostoglotov to the Kadmins telling about the cancer ward and of his hopes for the future. Throughout these chapters we receive glimpses into the minds of various characters and watch the progress of their cases and their relationships with each other. In Chapter 23, we meet Maxim Petrovich Chaly, an enthusiastic entrepreneur and middleman whose philosophy is "why not live well?" He makes friends with Rusanov. His philosophy becomes a matter for discussion. The relationship between Kostoglotov and Vera is further explored, and we see in detail his effect on her otherwise unromantic life. We meet Lev Leonidovich, an extremely competent, decent, hard-working surgeon who must constantly keep from offending his superior, the "senior doctor," an incompetent administrator who never misses a chance "to gain rewards and a whole range of special privileges" (353). More concerned than the other doctors about "the nature of our whole society" (366), Lev Leonidovich has recently and successfully resisted the medical bureaucracy during a public inquiry. Because Lev once worked in a prison camp, he and Kostoglotov find that they understand each other.

As the novel progresses, various cases are disposed of. Dyomka's leg is amputated and Asya's breast will have to be removed, and Solzhenitsyn shows how the two young people respond to these grisly facts. Rusanov's older son, Yuri, visits the ward, and we see that he is *not* going to be like his father. Shortly afterwards, Rusanov, unaware that he is terminally ill, is released from the hospital and driven home by his younger children, Lavrik and Maika, both of whom *are* going to be like their father. Ludmila Dontsova, worried about her own health, pays a call on aging Dr. Oreshchenkov, an old-fashioned man who has managed to maintain a private practice; he is against specialization, and he disapproves of the Soviet national health service and, by extension, the entire bureaucratic structure of his society. After considerable tension and misunderstanding, Kostoglotov realizes that Vera is preferable to Zoya, and for a time it appears that Vera's invitation to come to her apartment after his release is a signal that their love will blossom. In Chapter 31, "Idols of the Market Place," Kostoglotov and Shulubin have an important discussion about the nature of socialism. Again we are privy to Dontsova's thoughts as she makes her rounds. She is now fully aware of her own spreading cancer. Some of the patients sense her situation; others do not.

By Chapter 34 Kostoglotov is beginning to feel that the ward is "no longer his home" (473). Most of his fellow patients have been discharged, are dead, or are soon to die. He talks with Elizaveta Anatolyevna, an intelligent and well-mannered orderly whose husband has been in prison for years. They discuss her problems, and Oleg offers comfort. At the end of the chapter, at Shulubin's bedside, Oleg is reminded of a previous conversation in which the former professor had said:

> "Sometimes I feel quite distinctly that what is inside me is not all of me. There's something else, sublime, quite indestructible, some tiny fragment of the universal spirit. Don't you feel that?" (483)

And then in Chapter 35, in what seems to Oleg like "the morning of creation" (485), he is released from the hospital and moves slowly through the strange city where everything "was new and had to be understood afresh" (488). After several unusual experiences, including a visit to the zoo and an embarrassing incident in a department store, he decides to go to Vera's apartment—but she isn't home, and he is scared away. He goes to the train station, purchases a ticket for Ush-Terek, and writes Vera a farewell note. He leaves the city feeling good about having survived but also aware of anguish "in the deepest seat of his emotions" (522).

Although *Cancer Ward* has its intellectuals (Shulubin and the philosophy lecturer who looks like a bank manager), independent thinkers (Kostoglotov and Lev Leonidovich), and scientists (Vadim and some of the doctors), the novel is populated principally by a cross-section of Soviet citizens, most of whom have lived in (comparative) freedom; most have kept their eyes on the tasks immediately before them, and many know almost nothing about the Gulag network. Unlike the highly educated and professionally thoughtful prisoners in *The First Circle*, they are unused to discussing questions like those posed by the Tolstoy story, "What do men live by?" Their talk often stumbles along awkwardly, as if only recently, under the threat of death, have these questions come to matter. Now that they are at a crossroads, these people *need* to talk and to think, but they lack the background of a Lev Rubin, a Dimitri Sologdin, or even a Gleb Nerzhin; few of them are famous or notably expert in their fields, and

125

most know their own limitations. In all his fiction Solzhenitsyn deals indirectly with the question of what men live by, but in *Cancer Ward* the question sits directly on the surface: What do *ordinary* men, the mass of men, live by —men who are neither prisoners nor intellectuals?

Very early in the novel, the young Dyomka tells Kostoglotov that he would like to attend a university. Kostoglotov, whose miscellaneous education includes some university work, replies that that is fine but asks Dyomka to remember that "education doesn't make you smarter."

"So what does make you smarter?"
"Life, that's what" (21).

And when Dyomka asks Kostoglotov what is intelligence, the older man replies, "Trusting your eyes but not your ears" (21). Direct answers to direct questions. Kostoglotov goes on to offer Dyomka lessons in the first principles of stereometry, a subject in which Dyomka thinks he may be interested and which Kostoglotov has studied in the course of his varied experience. Kostoglotov's authority is quickly established in Dyomka's eyes and in our own. And a tone is set: the talk in *Cancer Ward* will be straightforward and low to the ground. Not that the inmates are necessarily unintelligent; on the contrary, much of the novel's energy comes from Solzhenitsyn's recognition that when ordinary people get together under these circumstances there is often a kind of competition among them to show how common-sensically smart they are. The reader is in the position of deciding who in fact (besides Kostoglotov) *does* know "life" well enough to be truly smart and who is capable of learning from the cancer ward experience itself, which is likely to be one's final experience.

In Chapter 8, "What Men Live By," we witness Yefrem Podduyev's awakening, one of the *Cancer Ward* equivalents to the many awakenings in *The First Circle*. "If it hadn't been for the grip of cancer on his throat, Yefrem Podduyev would have been a man in the prime of life"

(93). He is fifty. Up to now he has been tough as a "two-humped camel," capable of doing a "mountain of work" (93), a vigorous, lusty, selfish, he-man who constantly uses his tongue:

> With it he'd talked his way into pay he'd never earned, sworn blind he'd done things when he hadn't, stood bail for things he didn't believe in, howled at the bosses and yelled insults at the workers. With it he piled filth on everything most dear and holy, reveling in his trills like a nightingale. He told fat-ass stories but never touched politics. He sang Volga songs. He lied to hundreds of women scattered all over the place, that he wasn't married, that he had no children, that he'd be back in a week and they'd start building a house (94).

He has always managed to do what he wanted to, to have "a free life and money in his pocket" (95), and he has always known exactly "what was asked of a man," namely a "good trade" or a "good grip on life," both of which "would get you money" (96). If the narrator of *Cancer Ward* were a degree or two more strident and judgmental, we might be asked to condemn Yefrem for his self-centered obliviousness to anything but his own needs and emotions. His energy makes him interesting, but he is amoral, apparently without that innate sense of rectitude of so many uneducated peasants and workers in Solzhenitsyn's world (although there *is* a difference between a peripatetic worker like Podduyev and an uprooted peasant like Ivan Denisovich Shukhov or Spiridon). We could blame him for inadvertently aiding and abetting the enemy; that is, for supporting the State by devoting himself exclusively to material ends. As it is, however, the narrator is rather good-humored about Yefrem, possibly because up to now Yefrem has kept control of his own life and remained a free and uncommitted man in a country where it is difficult to avoid one kind of prison or another. That achievement is acknowledged.

But he has learned nothing in his lifetime which will

help prepare him to meet death. In the cancer ward he spends hours "running for help" (96), and it is not until Kostoglotov gives him a collection of short stories that he finds any means of getting outside himself. Yefrem had never been a reader; he had "lived his whole life without such a serious book ever coming his way" (99). Kotoglotov, who during the novel discovers that he is a natural teacher, would have been gratified by Yefrem's reaction to the first story he reads, the shortest one in the collection:

> He read it. He felt like thinking. He thought. He felt like reading the little story again. He did. He felt like thinking again. He thought again.
> It was the same with the second story (98).

This reads like a first-grade primer because, despite all the adventures and all the women, Yefrem is in many respects like a child. He has never before thought about anything that mattered. He hasn't had to. Instead, he has been "living" life, a working-man counterpart of Innokenty Volodin before *his* transformation into a thinking man. Even now Yefrem's awakening comes too late to open up any spectacular intellectual vistas. He does question his former assumptions about women (all they do is "cling") and admits that he is to blame for treating them badly. He begins to take seriously Tolstoy's idea that "people live not by worrying only about their own problems but by love of others" (104). But he does not have enough time left to practice or to test this idea—although he eventually asserts that the book is "very right" as long as "everyone started living by it at the same time" (205), which is easy to say and not quite the point anyway. Yefrem is a practical man and he does not intend to be taken advantage of even as his own hardened sensibility begins to melt.

The step-by-step process of beginning to think is mapped out carefully several times in *Cancer Ward* (as well as in *The First Circle* and *August 1914*), as if Sol-

128

zhenitsyn wishes to reemphasize whenever possible that a Man Thinking is rare on any social level and under any circumstances. Everyone believes, naturally, that he "thinks"—no mind is an empty jar—but Solzhenitsyn is concerned not with thinking-for-recreation (as intellectuals) or thinking-on-the-job (as engineers) but with a process which results in an individual's gaining a sobering new perception of life or a dawning sense that his previous self-conceptions were false. He continually suggests that it is difficult to think; people rarely do it unless they must and even then are usually unprepared; beware of ideologues and philosophizers who make the process seem easy. Because the dying Yefrem is, for the first time in his life, suffering and desperate, when he finally begins to think, he *is* prepared for the influx (almost like divine grace) of one new and exceedingly simple idea: Love exists and is important. It comes to him not as a revelation but as a dawning question—"Had he learned something new and did he want to live differently?" (204)— and yet it is enough to enable him to accept his own death with more dignity than we might have expected. He walks out of the novel on his feet. When Kostoglotov gives Yefrem his imprimatur and they shake hands, Yefrem grins and says, "When you're born, you wriggle; when you grow up, you run wild; when you die, that's your lot" (206). Had Yefrem continued to live, it is likely that he would have maintained this capacity to put things in perspective, to see further outside of himself than ever in the past.

A simple idea brings a significant change; a slight shift in the heart makes Yefrem's life different. Perhaps the best reason for calling Solzhenitsyn an optimistic writer is his belief that this *can* happen to a person. The right idea, the right book, or the right person at the right time can, like the sun moving out from behind a cloud, bring clarity to a man like Yefrem. It is a matter of readiness and being smart enough to recognize the truth when it hits you. It is not a matter of education. People need truth. A little goes a long way. And yet it is not until Yefrem gets cancer that he even knows what he has been missing or even feels the need for some kind of conceptual support for the final days of his life. Cancer forces him to be an unhappier and then, for a very short time, a better man. He is reminded as never before of a time years ago when his cruelty toward a group of prisoners he was supervising elicited the comment from one of them, "It'll be your turn to die one day" (204), and he even has an inkling of the existence of an immortal part of himself:

> He was getting used to the idea of his own death, as one does to the death of a neighbor. But whatever it was inside him that thought of Yefrem Podduyev's death as of a neighbor's—this, it seemed, ought not to die (204).

But, one might ask, so what? Yefrem's selfish life is over. He is not going to make amends to anyone at this late date; he is incapable of doing good. But Solzhenitsyn is apparently willing to risk melodrama with these death-bed illuminations in order to make us feel the pathos of Yefrem's one-dimensional wasted life. With his enormous energy, what a man he might have been had he discovered years earlier that there were people in the world besides himself. Yefrem is also used as an example of a practical and hedonistic man who *does* after all have an innate sense of rectitude, a blossoming soul, a predilection for "love." Solzhenitsyn rarely gives up on humanity; he redeems even his less admirable characters whenever he plausibly can do so.

It is Yefrem who introduces the ward at large to the question, what do men live by, and who serves as a gruff master of ceremonies for the discussion which follows. Not that he is as confident as he sounds as he solicits answers from each of the men around him. ("Anyone else? What do men live by? . . . Well? Come on . . . Well, big boy? . . . All right. Anybody else?" [102]) He is uncertain, concerned, honestly wondering if the others have an answer, but he doesn't want them to think that *he* really cares about such a serious intellectual question. Better to call it a "riddle" (101). Better to cajole them into giving answers. And none of them want to be *without* answers, either. Even though they, too, find the question difficult, they all manage to come up with crisp replies as though they had thought about the question every day of their lives. They haven't; most people don't; presumably we all should. Solzhenitsyn arranges it so that the men answer predictably, according to their own immediate sense of things. ("Uniforms and supplies," says Ahmadjan; "By their pay," says Turgan; "Professional skill," says Proshka; "Your homeland," says Sibgatov [101– 102].) But none of them, except for Rusanov, are as sure of themselves as they act. It is as if they are waiting for someone to offer a better answer than their own. And none of them are sophisticated enough to hedge, to say "It all depends on your point of view" (not that it really *does*, in Solzhenitsyn's terms). Their initial answers are bound to be based on self-interest (a kind of reflex action), but the more important effect of this scene is that it shows a concern for moral and ethical issues among men who ordinarily would not admit it.

One reason for their reluctance to take on these questions publicly is that there is always someone like Rusanov around to make them feel foolish. When Yefrem asks Rusanov the question, what do men live by, Rusanov's answer costs him nothing, not even a moment's hesitation:

> He barely looked up from the chicken. "There's no difficulty about that," he said. "Remember: people live by their ideological principles and by the interests of their society." And he bit off the sweetest piece of gristle in the joint (103).

Shortly afterwards, Rusanov asserts—he "spat the words out"—that the moral to the story which Yefrem reads is "nonsense" and "quite alien to us" and that love has "nothing to do with our sort of morality" (104). Rusanov may sound as though he has deliberated upon these matters, but he has not. All his opinions are second-hand, all his "knowledge" easy slogans and conventional orthodoxies. But his quick responses are intimidating, and his blithe appropriation of the words "us" and "our"—as though he is a spokesman for a Soviet national identity—can only confuse a man like Yefrem, who is unpracticed in such a discussion and would probably be the first to admit that he is unqualified to judge what is or is not "alien to us." Yefrem, however, because a part of him grudgingly clings to the soft word "love," because he is more interested in the point of the story than in who wrote it (he has never heard of Tolstoy), and because he is capable of learning, is in fact "smarter" than Rusanov even though he doesn't know it.

Solzhenitsyn never tires of showing that ordinary, intellectually unpretentious people, while easily bullied, are often potentially wiser than slogan-men like Rusanov. Protective of his newfound idea, Yefrem is "furious" that Rusanov "had almost guessed the answer" when he uses the phrase "the interests of society" (104). To Yefrem, "love of others" and "the interests of society" sound pretty much the same, and he is upset that such a "pipsqueak" as Rusanov already seems to know what he himself has only recently discovered. But we know that when Rusanov says "interests of society," he does not mean "love of others"; he does not know what he means. His willingness to blurt out these memorized phrases shows merely that he regards himself as a comfortable member of the Party, part of a secure elite. "Interests of society" is high-sounding, impersonal, and convenient; Rusanov, like Stalin in *The First Circle*, actually is frightened of the *people*. "Love of others" is fresher (at least to Yefrem), signifying that real live individuals, the ones you meet every day, even in places like the cancer ward, are the creatures you must live with and love. Presumably, if he had lived, Yefrem would have begun to act upon this simple fact. It seems unlikely that Rusanov, whose "in-

132

terests of society" is a way of putting real live people at a distance, will ever learn it.

Although a fool, Rusanov mouths a line supported by far better men than himself. The ever-present issue of individualism vs. collectivism surfaces in *Cancer Ward* and is discussed passionately by this cross-section of people, as if, under the circumstances they all are in, the issue is not as complicated or as undiscussible as it often seems. As David Burg and George Feifer point out, Solzhenitsyn's concern for the individual may seem "unremarkable" to us in the West but constitutes "a ringing dissent . . . from one of the most fundamental axioms of the collectivist philosophy which permeated Soviet society and dominated its literature."[3] Solzhenitsyn himself has felt obliged to remark, as though it were news, that an "individual's life is not always the same as society's. The collective does not always assist the individual. . . . A person is a physiological and spiritual being before he becomes a member of society."[4] And in *Cancer Ward* he has Kostoglotov say:

> "Because what do we keep telling a man all his life? 'You're a member of the collective! You're a member of the collective!' That's right. But only while he's alive. When the time comes for him to die, we release him from the collective. He may be a member, but he has to die alone. It's only he who is saddled with the tumor, not the whole collective" (137).

That the collective always promises more than it can possibly deliver is a commonplace in Solzhenitsyn's fictional world but becomes especially apparent in *Cancer Ward*. The hospital itself is an arm of the collectivized society, but unlike the sharashka or the labor camp, it is a "free" and benevolent institution and people willingly place themselves in its hands, hoping against hope that it will solve the greatest problem of their life. Sometimes it does. Kostoglotov, however, in Chapter 11 tells his fellow ward members that "we shouldn't behave like rabbits and put our complete trust in doctors" and goes on to introduce the concept of "self-induced healing" (133), as if to suggest that most men agree too quickly to yield up their own powers of self-help. He sounds a trifle silly and complacent when he talks in this vein (he himself is euphoric over his own rapid improvement and rather likes the sound of his own voice), and yet it is undeniably exciting to entertain the possibility that one's cancer could be cured by oneself. If a person could do this, he could do almost anything. He would be fearless.

But most of the men Kostoglotov is lecturing in Chapter 11 *are* afraid, and they know that he is telling them "a fairy tale" (133). They listen to him because they are desperate for any kind of good news. Only Yefrem Podduyev goes so far as to speculate that for self-induced healing to work one needs "a clear conscience" (133), revealing again how much his new Tolstoy-derived knowledge has affected him. The entire discussion of self-induced healing may seem dangerously misleading, but Kostoglotov (and Solzhenitsyn behind him) is continually trying to resurrect idealism among the hard-bitten and to reopen questions which the committed materialist-collectivists think were closed off long ago. When Yefrem mentions "conscience," Rusanov calls it "idealistic nonsense," but then Kostoglotov intervenes with his teacherly "You've hit the nail on the head, Yefrem. Well done! Anything can happen, we don't know a damn thing" (133). He goes on to summarize an article he read about the relationship between potassium and sodium salts existing in a "blood-and-brain barrier" at the base of the skull and how in a man with a cheerful, staunch "attitude of mind" a surplus of sodium builds up in the barrier "and no illness whatever can make him die!" (134) Solzhenitsyn is probably more inclined to believe this than we are, but the important point is not the validity of this particular theory so much as Kostoglotov's statement that "Anything can happen, we don't know a damn thing." An ordinary man's hunch that bad conscience is a cause of cancer may turn out to be as valid a method of identifying causes of cancer as the methods used by the medical community.

Kostoglotov also wants his pupils to admit that mankind is not nearly as knowledgeable as some of its experts pretend, that profound mysteries remain, that pat "scientific" explanations of human behavior ought to be regarded skeptically. His information about a person's internal chemistry sounds scientific enough to keep Rusanov quiet for a while and also causes Vadim, the young geologist, to give the theory his approval (the "physiology of optimism," he labels it), but when Rusanov sees that Kostoglotov is really more interested in moral solutions to human problems than in scientific solutions, he explodes: "There are questions on which a definite opinion has been established, and they are no longer open to discussion" (135). And of course it is that very attitude which Kostoglotov is against. At one point Rusanov actually tells Yefrem, who is lugubriously wallowing in memories of his former evil deeds, that "you've disarmed yourself ideologically. You keep harping on about that stupid moral perfection!" (135)

Rusanov's foolishness is indisputable whenever he appears in the novel. Solzhenitsyn is even willing to risk making him a stereotype self-important Communist Party lackey in order to emphasize his ostrich-like mind. Lev Rubin in *The First Circle* was also a committed Communist, but he was a good and unusual man, as well. Rusanov is neither. Everything he says, feels, and sees is based on formulas provided by Communist ideology. He accepts what the experts in any field tell him; whatever is official is right. Because loyalty to the collective and to the Party has made him materially comfortable, he has no use for any other guide, especially that of moral conscience, which suggests that the individual is more important than the collective. For Rusanov everything worth knowing is already known, and like the majority of Establishment Communists in Solzhenitsyn's world he is the furthest thing possible from a revolutionary. He is deathly afraid of new ideas; he is deeply reactionary. For Kostoglotov the world is still full of possibility and undiscovered territory, and a single individual can, indeed *must*, find his own way through its swamps to the high ground.

As we can infer from *The First Circle* and as is unmistakable in his play *Candle in the Wind*, the former physics teacher Solzhenitsyn is capable of questioning the primacy of science and technology in modern life. In *Candle in the Wind* he has the forty-year-old mathematician Alex Coriel say, "I'm suspicious . . . about all science in general. Science has successfully proved that it's very good at serving the cause of tyranny."[5] Despite his resemblance to Solzhenitsyn himself, Coriel is a simple character; indeed, the entire play reads like an outline, a reminder to himself, of ideas and situations which Solzhenitsyn knew would have to be developed more fully elsewhere. Alex's friend, Philip Radagise, also an ex-prisoner but also a worshipper of science, resents Alex's moral and philosophical earnestness and, like a weary reader of Solzhenitsyn's works, tells him to "stop shoving your prison sentence into everyone's face" (51). But that prison sentence *does* give Alex the authority to be ingenuously heretical: "Why do we need science at all?" he asks. "I get the answer that it's interesting, it's a process that cannot be halted, it's connected with the production forces of the economy" (111). Although Philip's answer to Alex's question is not as stupid as we are invited to conclude (all "the material goods we possess on our planet, our entire civilization, our entire culture—everything was created by science, everything!" [52]), it is characteristic of the play's simplification and polarization of its important issues. In both *Candle in the Wind* and *The First Circle*, Solzhenitsyn makes it easy for us to accept his skepticism of science by having the scientists themselves work for institutions (the sharashka and the biocybernetics laboratory) dedicated to goals which involve direct manipulation and control of human beings.

But in *Cancer Ward* the uses to which science and technology are put make blanket condemnations of science more difficult. The doctors, while not themselves pure scientists, do believe in science; and the x-ray machine is a dramatic example of a technological innovation which can save or prolong lives. Why do we need science? If not to produce material goods, why then, one might reasonably answer, we need it to save lives. Those doctors we get to know best are not ingenious theoreticians pursuing their profession because it is merely "interesting." They sincerely want to help people, and long stretches of the novel show Gangart, Dontsova, and Lev Leonidovich, even though overworked, taking a personal interest in the lives of their patients. As a part of the Soviet bureaucracy, the hospital staff is subject to the dehumanizing regulations, administrative pressures, and forms of intimidation which we have come to expect in all the institutions of Solzhenitsyn's world (see Chapter 7, where we follow Dr. Dontsova through a typical day), and yet when they must, most of the doctors and staff members can work their way through the labyrinths of that bureaucracy.

When a person knows that his work is useful, a rare satisfaction in Solzhenitsyn, it is easier for him to muster the strength to do that work. With images of their patients' sufferings and hopes constantly in their minds, the doctors, like competent soldiers on the front lines, devise ways to do their jobs even though they are underequipped, bound by restrictions, and under surveillance by higher authorities. In Chapter 1, when Rusanov's awful wife tries to bribe the matron Mita to arrange for special attention for her husband, Mita instantly feels "cold all over" and replies, "We don't do that sort of thing here" (6). As we know from other Solzhenitsyn works, especially *Ivan Denisovich*, "that sort of thing" is a way of life in the Soviet Union, but from the beginning the cancer ward is presented as an institution with unusually high ethical standards. While some members of the medical staff *are* bribable, incompetent, and materialistic, including the clinic's senior doctor, Nizamutdin Bahramovich, Solzhe-

137

nitsyn goes out of his way in *Cancer Ward* to enumerate individual acts of kindness by other members of the staff, as if to suggest that the practice of medicine has not yet yielded to the pervasive impersonality that is the mark of the bureaucracy in general.

It can be claimed, in other words, that *Cancer Ward*, set two years after the death of Stalin when it appeared that the strictures were loosening in the Soviet Union, is about an institution and a profession which is more good than evil, and which for the most part uses science and technology properly. Even the most dogmatic anti-Soviet and anti-modernist would have to admit that the cancer ward is a progressive institution in both the moral and scientific sense—far from perfect, but the best sort of institution the Soviet Union can hope for. In the end, this may be the conclusion we are meant to reach. But the boldest feature of the novel is the extent to which Solzhenitsyn resists this conclusion without exactly undermining it. The painful fact is that despite all the technology and good will in the world, this or any cancer clinic has only limited success against cancer—but we know that, and still we approve of the clinic's continuing effort to conquer this dreadful disease. Nevertheless, the novel poses the question of whether the price we pay for our faith in the miracles of modern medicine (and by extension our faith in other miracles to be wrought by science and technology) is not too high.

In Chapter 6, where Kostoglotov tells Ludmila Dontsova of his medical history, he draws an analogy between the hospital and the prison camps. Even though he voluntarily put himself in the hospital's hands, he complains that "once again I become a grain of sand, just as I was in the camp. Once again nothing *depends* on me" (74). Part of Kostoglotov's fascination as a character is that his excess of pent-up energy allows him to fight several battles at once. He wants to be an individualist in a collectivist society. He wants to be a thoughtful and moral man, but he is burning with lust, steaming with grievances and resentment, not always in control of his temper

138

(though, usually, outwardly cheerful). He wants to live in a homemade, do-it-yourself world when the actual world seems suited only for experts and specialists; and of course he wishes to be healthy and alive, yet he is battling cancer. Dontsova, who quite correctly does not regard herself as an oppressor, naturally resists his somewhat unfair attempt to link the cancer ward with prison. She questions his logic: "Twelve sessions of x-rays have turned you from a corpse into a living human being. How dare you attack your treatment?" (75) Dontsova does not usually take a how-dare-you tone with anyone, but it is a mark of Kostoglotov's character that he has manipulated her into a position where she must explain and justify herself and her treatment. Most patients, most people, are conditioned to take her expertise for granted —and that nearly universal habit of deferring to the experts is, in Kostoglotov's view, part of the trouble with his entire society. To Dontsova's attack on his logic, Kostoglotov replies:

> "After all, man is a complicated being, why should he be explainable by logic? Or for that matter by economics? Or physiology? Yes, I did come to you as a corpse, and I begged you to take me in, and I lay on the floor by the staircase. And therefore you make the logical deduction that I came to you to be saved *at any price*. There isn't anything in the world for which I'd agree to pay any price!" (75)

It is a familiar cry in Solzhenitsyn. If the process of being cured—or being "rehabilitated" or made "happy"—means taking away every vestige of personal choice, of becoming a passive patient upon whom the experts can work, then Kostoglotov would rather die.

But the reader has more information about Dontsova than does Kostoglotov and knows that while she is fascinated by the problems of his special case, she does not regard him only as a case. She likes him, and she wants to see *him*—Kostoglotov the individual, this man in

139

front of her—cured. Even though she defends her position vigorously (she insists that doctors *are* entitled to the right of deciding for someone else—"doctors above all" [77]), we sense that she is not hopelessly enamored with her own authority or her own ingenuity. Even her faith in modern medical science—her treatment of Kostoglotov was "highly recommended for this particular type of cancer by the most up-to-date authorities" (80)—is not, we soon discover, unshakable. There are moments, yes, when she seems too much like some of those dedicated scientists and engineers in *The First Circle* who fail to see the moral and political implications of their work. Her ignorance of medical malpractice in the Gulag network is distressing, and so is her tendency to give fearful respect to those above her in authority, which at one point causes her prison-wise colleague, Lev Leonidovich, to rebuke her for being rather doggedly unaware of "the nature of our whole society" (366). Because she is a celebrity in the cancer ward, which is a world of its own, she could easily become a petty tyrant, one of those stolid medical bureaucrats whose secure position helps to dry up their consciences, but Solzhenitsyn does not allow that to happen. He gives Dontsova an active conscience.

For some time she has experienced a "gnawing feeling of deep-rooted and unpardonable guilt" (88) as a result of the discovery that she and others like her have been causing unforeseen damage to people ("X ray radiation had seemed such a straightforward, reliable, and foolproof method, such a magnificent achievement of modern medical technique" [87]). However reluctant to admit it, she knows that Kostoglotov *is* right to question his treatment, and she herself begins to reflect on the wider implications of his challenge to a doctor's absolute right to treat:

> Once you begin to think like that, to doubt every method scientifically accepted today simply because it might be discredited or abandoned in the future, then goodness knows where you'd end up. After all there were cases on record of death from aspirin. A man might take the

140

first aspirin of his life and die of it! By that reasoning it became impossible to treat anyone. By that reasoning all the daily advantages of medicine would have to be sacrificed.

It was a universal law: everyone who *acts* breeds both good and evil. With some it's more good, with others more evil (88).

Although it is not credible that Kostoglotov is the first person to awaken these thoughts in Dontsova, it is important for Solzhenitsyn to have an Establishment doctor inadvertently open the question of whether slavish dedication to "scientifically accepted" methods is effective, let alone right. Dontsova is committed to the truism that science is always making progress; Solzhenitsyn, with the example of the dangerous x-ray machine for support, wants his readers to take a second look at the supposed "daily advantages of medicine" and to question the more general assumption that all science and technology are for man's advantage. What Dontsova is also doing here, almost without knowing it herself, is applying moral terms to a process which many people regard as morally neutral. She has been a highly successful healer, but she has also made mistakes and "until the day she died she would always remember the handful of poor devils who had fallen under the wheels" (88). That lingering memory saves her, and sets her apart from those doctors whose attitude toward their losses is more cavalier and realistic, who would shrug their shoulders and say that you cannot win them all.

It may be that the x-ray machine is dangerous, but Dontsova, even though suffering from radiation sickness herself, does *not* repudiate x-ray therapy. It is also true that the "barbarous bombardment of heavy quanta, soundless and unnoticed by the assaulted tissues" (66) has given Kostoglotov back his desire for life and made it possible for him to challenge Dontsova in the first place. And even at the end of the novel, Kostoglotov *does* decide, after much uncertainty, to accept the therapeutic program the hospital devises for him (at the cost of his sexual potency). Solzhenitsyn knows as well as we do that the modern hospital, whose staff and equipment when properly used epitomize the best of applied science and technology, is for the most part useful and necessary, but he wants to establish a situation in which even this almost sacrosanct institution can be challenged. Unlike prison camps, hospitals justify their own existence; they need not be abolished. But he does use the hospital and all it connotes as a vehicle to suggest that worship of science in general has gone too far.

For many American readers this case need not be made. We have always had voices in this country warning us against the ravages of technology and the misuse of science, and even if these voices are in the minority, they do not always go unconsidered nor are they always held in contempt. But under a government like that of the Soviet Union, whose very existence depends on the idea that improved material circumstances will make men happy and equal and that only through the deliberate application of scientific principles can this material improvement come about, to challenge science *at all* is significant. Indeed, it is heresy. Solzhenitsyn's heroes always hesitate to align themselves with institutions which are based on the proposition that science and social science are the only means of discovering truth, a proposition which is much more widely held in the Soviet Union than in the United States. For Solzhenitsyn, who believes that the ultimate reality is spiritual rather than material, the case against the worship of science cannot be made often enough. It is one of his ways of exhorting his readers to think for themselves. It is of course stupid to be "against" science, but it is not stupid to think carefully, as Kostoglotov does, about its implications; he "could not give himself unreservedly to the treatment until he had grasped for himself the theory behind it and so was able to believe in it" (66).

Even though most of us would agree that in some areas of life, in some countries, a technological saturation point appears to have been reached (transportation, electronic communication, weaponry, probably not medicine, certainly not food production), and even though we may occasionally show interest in resurrecting simpler forms of technology, as readers of *Cancer Ward* we are likely to be jolted by this passage:

> Kostoglotov had something in reserve—a secret medicine, a mandrake root from Issyk Kul. There was a motive behind his wish to go back to his place in the woodlands—he wanted to treat himself with the root. Because he had the root, he'd really only come to the cancer clinic to see what it was like (79).

A mandrake root? *Is* Kostoglotov thinking carefully? Is Solzhenitsyn? One suddenly loses confidence in the hero. Eventually, however, we see that this passage and others like it are Solzhenitsyn's way of suggesting that important discoveries can be and have been made by ordinary people with improper credentials who use unscientific methods; it is as if he has in mind as a target those who would glibly deny the power of discovery to anyone outside the mainstream of established institutions.

It turns out that Kostoglotov went into the mountains not far from his place of exile and got the medicine from an old man who settled there early in the century, an "honest-to-goodness medicine man who goes out, collects the roots and works out the doses himself" (227). When he explains all this to Vera Gangart, she is appalled (the root contains aconite, a deadly poison; the old man gave Kostoglotov a "handful of root" which he measured by eye [227]). Kostoglotov says to her, "To be honest, I'm not convinced it was the X rays alone that got rid of my pain. I' might have been the root as well" (226). In Solzhenitsyn's own case such a root received from just such a man did in fact relieve his pain and arrest his tumor until he could get to the hospital at Tashkent, but in *Cancer Ward* he has Kostoglotov show some uncertainty

143

about it.[6] "I don't suppose you believe it works?" he asks Vera.

> "No, of course I don't. It's just a lot of dark superstition and playing some games with death. I believe in systematic science, practically tested. That's what I was taught and that's the way all oncologists think" (228).

It may seem that the issue is clear: x-rays and systematic science versus mandrake roots and measuring by eye. But I think Solzhenitsyn is resisting only the absolute certainty we hear in Vera's voice. The hospital *does* help Kostoglotov more than the medicine man did, but the latter's old-fashioned methods have *something* to be said for them. It is a matter of degree and of tone. Although Vera is not habitually arrogant, and although much more is at stake in their conversation than mere medicine, on this issue she assumes the haughty tone of the expert, and she does seem a little foolish. Ordinarily she is humble and sensitive, too sharp in her quiet way to want to dismiss complicated human endeavors as "a lot of dark superstition." People have lived on this earth long before the modern Soviet state was born; not everything those people knew is obsolete. Kostoglotov, who is falling in love with Vera, does not want her to assume an attitude which is unworthy of her.

In *Cancer Ward* and elsewhere, whenever he can publicize the effectiveness of the old ways, Solzhenitsyn does. Yefrem Podduyev, trying to discover how to die, remembers how the "old folk" back home did it:

> They didn't puff themselves up or fight against it or brag that they weren't going to die—they took death calmly. They didn't stall squaring things away, they prepared themselves quietly and in good time, deciding who should have the mare, who the foal, who the coat and who the boots. And they departed easily, as if they were just moving into a new house. None of them would be scared by cancer. Anyway, none of them got it (97).

Measured against this passage, the cancer ward seems a rather silly institution, dedicated to hasty and mostly futile attempts to cure people of a strictly modern illness. Yefrem is not the most reliable of historians, but through him Solzhenitsyn is nevertheless encouraging the speculation that among spiritually strong people who live according to older rhythms cancer is unknown and dignity automatic.

Then there is the example of Dr. Maslennikov, an "old pre-Revolutionary country doctor" who discovered that a tea made from *chaga*—a birch tree fungus—keeps the peasants in his district free from cancer (141). When Kostoglotov tells the ward about Maslennikov everyone listens, including Rusanov, who suddenly acquires an interest in this "simple Russian folk remedy" (142). But it is also Rusanov, the novel's spokesman for Stalinist orthodoxy, who must ask, "But is this method officially recognized? . . . Has it been approved by a government department?" (142) No, it hasn't. And it is not likely to be. Although in theory a government of the people, the state has become so inflexible that it is unprepared to recognize remedies (for anything) which come to it from such people as peasants and pre-Revolutionary doctors. Maslennikov is forced to conduct what amounts to an underground campaign to make his discovery known.

A far more extensive commentary on medical modernism is Solzhenitsyn's portrait of seventy-five-year-old Dr. Oreshchenkov (Chapter 30). It is ironic that when Dr. Dontsova realizes she needs help with her own illness, she turns to a man whose entire way of life is a challenge to Soviet orthodoxies, who seems like a small-town Republican doctor in Kansas. Against enormous odds, Dr. Oreshchenkov has managed to maintain a private practice; he is against specialization; he wants to be available to "any passer-by" (416); he questions the so-called free universal national health service (it offers "depersonalized treatment" and its costs are merely hidden [423]); he reminds Dontsova of something she is in danger of forget-

145

ting (except in Kostoglotov's case), that each patient should be treated as an individual, "a subject on his own" (425); he prefers medicine as it was practiced before the Revolution, when the family physician served also as a family guide and counselor; and despite being himself an excellent radiologist (he was Dontsova's teacher), he says:

"You know I worked for twenty years before X rays were invented. And, my dear, you should have seen the diagnoses I made! It's like when you have an exposure meter or a watch, you completely lose the knack of estimating exposure by eye or judging time by instinct. When you don't have them, you soon acquire the trick" (418).

As he often does with off-beat characters whose ideas he supports, Solzhenitsyn gives Dr. Oreshchenkov a flaw or two—he is garrulous, somewhat dogmatic, a little patronizing. One could argue, moreover, that he has retreated from the real world or that his old-fashioned life in his "one-story house with a small garden" (412) mirrors the author's own longing for what he imagines to be that simpler and more deliberate form of existence which was possible fifty years before. But Solzhenitsyn takes pains to show that Dr. Oreshchenkov's way of life *is* credible, if rare, in time present. It is true that he has avoided a measure of official persecution by having been lucky enough to save the lives of important people; even so, his present "unhindered life" has not been easily gained and came to him only after the age of sixty-five (417). Dr. Oreshchenkov is not an escapee from reality. He is a man whose practical usefulness to people is recognized by some of them even though so much about him seems "old":

Dr. Oreshchenkov's house was guarded by a wooden-slatted door, alongside which stood an old-fashioned front door with a brass handle and heavy pyramid-

146

shaped panels. In houses like these the old doors were usually nailed up and one entered by the new door. But here the two stone steps that led up to the old door were not overgrown with grass and moss. There was a copper plate with sloping calligraphic writing on it. "Dr. D. T. Oreshchenkov" it read, and it was polished as brightly as it had been in the old days. The electric bell was set in a little cup. It did not look unused (414).

He still has patients. They come to him not because they wish to sip the tea and pet the dog of a quaint old man but because he is wise and competent. He is obviously smarter than Dontsova. His way of life is a form of heroism, and he stands as an example of someone who is effective in the present largely because he *does* cling to certain old-fashioned ways and beliefs.

Another feature of Dr. Oreshchenkov's portrait is that his house and manner (as opposed to his ideas on various subjects or even his expertise as a physician) meet a need in Dontsova which is also felt by a great many other Solzhenitsyn characters as well. This is a need for a quiet refuge, a private place in which one can (temporarily) escape from responsibility (and from various forms of surveillance). As soon as Dontsova sinks "deep into a soft armchair," she feels

almost confident that in this room only the best possible decisions could be taken. The burden of permanent responsibility, the burden of administration, the burden of choosing what she ought to do with her life, had been lifted from her shoulders at the coat rack in the corridor. Now she was deep in the armchair her problems had finally collapsed. Calm and relaxed, she let her eyes travel slowly round the room which, of course, she knew of old. It touched her to see the old marble washstand basin in the corner, not a modern washbasin but one with a bucket underneath it. It was all covered, though, and very clean (414).

On the perimeters of Solzhenitsyn's world are a number

of places like this (Matryona's house, for example, or the Kadmins' in Ush-Terek), repositories of dignity, wisdom, and calm, indicators of what life can be like among people not totally committed to modernization. The problems which exist in these out-of-the-way places seem as natural and inevitable as rainstorms when compared to the problems of those other confined spaces—prisons, wards, foxholes, high-rise apartment buildings—which are the centers of action in most of Solzhenitsyn's world. There, the space is overcrowded, unprivate, brightly lit, often under surveillance. All of Solzhenitsyn's novels have several characters for whom that overcrowded space is a source of frustration and pressure, and so when, as in Dontsova's case here, one suddenly finds himself in some unexpected circle of calm with a person he can trust absolutely, it is a rare gift. In a society committed to socialism, to defending public over private welfare, to confraternity, to the idea of people pulling the oars together, always together, the impulse for privacy is not given enthusiastic sanction. Dr. Oreshchenkov's house is not just a symbol of "the old days" (413), but a vehicle to help Solzhenitsyn show how infrequently people like Dontsova *can* relax and give themselves up to old-fashioned peace and quiet in some cozy place where they can say what is really on their minds. Again, it is a matter of degree. There are not enough of these refuges; there should be more of them; and there easily could be. This is not Solzhenitsyn's nostalgia speaking; it is his knowledge of what people actually need.

Although his very existence is reason for hope, it is also true that Dr. Oreshchenkov grew up in an earlier time and now his life is nearly over. What about hope for the future? Solzhenitsyn always poses the question and always, eventually, gives an affirmative answer. In *Cancer Ward*, as elsewhere, he pins this hope on the fact that there are still people left with the right values, for whom material goods, power, and self-indulgence are not everything. Sixteen-year-old Dyomka is among this group. But

148

Solzhenitsyn also puts Dyomka to the test, as if he well knows how the cultivation of moral superiority can also be a form of self-indulgence, not to mention an almost comically frail defense against certain overwhelming forces of contemporary life (what force does a "good" man, or do a thousand good men, have in comparison to a nuclear power plant or, for that matter, a single x-ray machine?). Dyomka's story also gives Solzhenitsyn a chance to explore one of his favorite subjects, the younger generation, about which he seems to have two general ideas: (1) The Soviet Establishment *has* succeeded in erasing from that generation's consciousness all old-fashioned standards of belief and behavior, and (2) One can always find young people like Dyomka around.

Dyomka's mother became a whore and rejected him at an early age; he has never had enough to eat; he is now about to have his leg amputated. His suffering has already helped to make him an apprentice truth-seeker who is predisposed to spiritual enlightenment, but for a long time he does not know where to turn. He wants to learn about life but he cannot keep up with the latest official views of its nature; he would like someone to show him "a little pity" but he had "read and heard that pity is a humiliating feeling: whether you pity or are pitied" (120); and because he is a resident of the men's ward, it is important for him to try to "behave like a man" (120), not a child in search of a comforting mother. But such comfort does come, anyway, when he is noticed by old Aunt Styofa, to whom eventually he tells his life story. "No one had ever listened to Dyomka so attentively and with such sympathy" (120).

This modest but humane act of taking Dyomka seriously makes Aunt Styofa one of several minor characters in *Cancer Ward* whose presence in the world seems a gift to it. Kindness is always important, but it is especially important in an uncertain life-and-death situation, for which few people have had any practice. Although in this particular cancer ward people do become interested in the ultimate questions, the nature of this disease also makes most of them fearful and self-absorbed, and when coaxed out of that depression by another's interest in them (or even by the smile of a passing medical attendant), they realize they are not dead yet. In the shadow of death a humane act is like medicine.

Aunt Styofa is kind to Dyomka not because she herself is lonely and needs someone to mother (her sons and daughters visit her often) but because kindness is an integral part of her life. Although there is no reason to assume that she acts solely out of her sense of Christian duty, she *is* a Christian, and that fact is important. She is another of those apparently anachronistic figures, a wrinkled old grandmother, whom Solzhenitsyn uses to question the prevailing Soviet sensibility, which is a version of the "modern" sensibility in whatever country it appears. When Styofa's relatives bring her things to eat, she "would call Dyomka out of his ward and slip an egg or a pastry into his hand" (122). Her life is regulated according to the Orthodox calendar (Shrovetide follows Meat Week, the Great Fast follows Shrovetide, and so forth). She is what could easily be called an unthinking believer, absolutely certain that "God sees everything" (121).

And Dyomka is attracted to Aunt Styofa's words in spite of his earlier ideologically impeccable education:

Ever since he had been in the first class, before he could read or write, Dyomka had been taught, knew for certain and fully understood that religion is a drug, a three-time reactionary dogma, of benefit only to swindlers. Because of it working people in some places had been unable to free themselves from exploitation. But as soon as they got rid of religion, they would take up arms and free themselves. And Aunt Styofa with her funny calendar, with the word "God" always on her lips, with her carefree smile even in that gloomy clinic, and her pastry, was obviously a thoroughly reactionary figure (122–3).

Although it sometimes seems so, Solzhenitsyn is not suggesting that everyone imitate Aunt Styofa (or Spiridon in *The First Circle*, or other old-fashioned people in his work), but he is urging that we not dismiss her or be so quick to label her beliefs "reactionary dogma." While many fanatically dogmatic and cruel people call themselves Christians, Aunt Styofa is a true Christian, kind and loving, rare characteristics in Soviet society as Solzhenitsyn portrays it. Moreover, her notion of submitting to God implies the existence of mysteries beyond human understanding and scientific methodology, a point Solzhenitsyn insists upon whenever he can. Neither Solzhenitsyn nor Kostoglotov, his primary spokesman in *Cancer Ward*, is *rejecting* human methodologies in favor of passive acceptance of the status quo (Kostoglotov himself is the leading exponent in *Cancer Ward* of self-induced healing), yet both of them believe that human reasoning has limits. Indeed, when an entire society is asked to believe that all problems can be solved and all questions ultimately answered, then that society is vulnerable to the tyranny of those claiming to be the problem-solvers and question-answerers. Some say that progress cannot happen without a powerful minority firmly in charge, but such an idea is not voiced in Solzhenitsyn's work (for one thing, he has less faith in conventional ideas of progress than most people do). But, one may ask, doesn't Aunt Styofa's religion keep her intellectually imprisoned? Not significantly, no. Believing in the authority of ultimate mystery is certainly comforting, but it is also humbling; in Solzhenitsyn's work truly religious people are never complacent, never convinced of their own infallibility or perfectability, and are certain only that God is ultimately in charge. Although rarely members of the intelligentsia, his religious characters are clear-sighted and minister unto immediate human needs, whereas the administrators and bureaucrats who value "objectivity" and the developing historical process almost always overlook immediate human needs and take their comfort in glib formulas like those which comprised Dyomka's early education. In *Gulag II*, in a poem outlining his own religious history, Solzhenitsyn includes a stanza about his period as an atheist:

Bookish subtleties sparkled brightly,
Piercing my arrogant brain,
The secrets of the world were . . . in my grasp,
Life's destiny . . . as pliable as wax (614).

In all his work, truly wise and experienced people learn to reject this sophomoric attitude.

In *Cancer Ward* Dyomka and Aunt Styofa do not discuss religion in any depth. Her kindness toward him simply makes it impossible to reject her words; she does not seem a "swindler" to him at all. What happens to Dyomka here happens elsewhere in Solzhenitsyn. When an extraordinarily decent person is also a solid believer in a creed that one may not believe in oneself, one tends to take a second look at that creed. Solzhenitsyn repeatedly suggests that any creed with a spiritual dimension is likely to make people more humane, and in the daily life of ordinary people humane acts make a difference. The majority of the orthodox Communists in his work, while officially committed to humane action, rarely make it a habit to *act* humanely (Lev Rubin in *The First Circle* is a notable exception)—and that is proof enough of the limitations of the attitudes fostered by the Soviet form of Marxist-Leninism. In the camps, the prisons, and the cancer ward, a man's actions count, not his theories, and true Christians in Solzhenitsyn's works practice what they preach (and, as for that, rarely preach).

For a sixteen-year-old boy, however, the true test of character is not merely the nature of his response to a wrinkled old Christian but the nature of his response to a beautiful, sexually interested female of his own age, and so Solzhenitsyn brings Asya into the narrative. One of the unusual aspects of *Cancer Ward* is that it investigates the values of several women of different ages who are at turning points in their lives, and Asya is the female representative of a generation of teenagers for whom there is apparently little hope. Asya has the wrong values. But among the things that keep any Solzhenitsyn work alive is that moral issues and spiritual questions often fade into insignificance in the presence of certain almost irresistible physical and material facts. For a hungry prisoner, an extra bowl of gruel is one of these facts. For Dyomka, one of those facts is Asya, who reminds him of "a film star" (123); she is so beautiful that he hardly dares look at her. Under ordinary circumstances she would be out of his class. Naive Dyomka, whose reaction against his mother's promiscuity has made him shy of the opposite sex, at first idealizes Asya as a "delicate yellow-haired angel" (131) and wants only the privilege of talking to her, but by the end of their first conversation he finds that "the little girl had knocked him clean off all he had held fast to for years" (131), including, presumably, the recent influence of Aunt Styofa.

What is the source of Asya's power? She is beautiful. She is brazen. She awakens Dyomka's sexual interest. Just as Aunt Styofa's kindness gave her creed authority in Dyomka's eyes, so does Asya's "cheerful healthiness" (129) and physicality make Dyomka want "to agree with everything she said in spite of his own beliefs" (129). Solzhenitsyn wants us to see that Asya is the end product of an education in materialism and hardly an "angel." (She is sitting in the clinic's Communist Party reading room which contains a larger-than-life bronze bust of Stalin.) She believes in money, fun, status, in being up-to-date, and in the doctrine that life "is for happiness" (128). She equates sex and love. "The earlier you start," she explains, "the more exciting it is. . . . Why wait? It's the atomic age!" (131) Despite the foolishness of much of her chatter ("Asya had an answer for everything" [128]), she makes Dyomka forget the pain in his leg, and for the first time in his life he begins to regard the sex act "as innocent before the whole world, unstained, capable of outweighing all the evil on earth" (130).

Because heretofore Dyomka has been preoccupied with "social problems" (126) and truth, it is tempting to

153

say that Asya is just what he needs, and that is partly correct, for he *is* a bore, as serious-minded truth-seekers tend to be. But even though sex is often celebrated in Solzhenitsyn, especially in *Cancer Ward*, it is never among the highest values—indeed, it is something that one *can* do without, if one must—and Dyomka has been misled if he continues to believe that it can "outweigh all the evil on earth." To lose onself in sex, to allow oneself to become a self-indulgent pleasure-seeker, is to become blind and stupid, and perhaps to end up like the orderly who sits there in the reading room with Dyomka and Asya enthusiastically eating sunflower seeds, spitting out the seeds without "any help from her hands" (124), and who with her heavy build and large mouth is compared to Stalin.

Asya recommends promiscuity because it is fun. "Life is for happiness," she says, and while most of us see the limitations of this view, we also know that it is fairly common, especially among teenagers, and probably would not hold it against Asya to the extent Solzhenitsyn does. The shallowness of young people is an easy target. But Solzhenitsyn is looking at Asya from a perspective colored by his years as a prisoner, during which time he saw people corrupted and broken because, as he says in *Gulag II*, they believed in

> That pitiful ideology which holds that "human beings are created for happiness," an ideology which is done in by the first blow of the work assigner's cudgel. . . .
>
> Those people became corrupted in camp who before camp had not been enriched by any morality at all or by any spiritual upbringing. (This is not at all a theoretical matter—since during our glorious half-century millions of them grew up.) (626)

And in 1955 they continue to grow up. Asya is one of them, and she is dangerous. Of course it is also true that if she were ugly, she would not be dangerous, at least not to Dyomka.

But the next time we see them together (Chapter 28), things have changed (Dyomka's leg has been amputated, Asya's breast is about to be removed). Dyomka's earlier predilection for seeking out what really matters has allowed him to reconcile himself to his altered condition without despairing (to submit, as Aunt Styofa might say). He is thinking "pleasant thoughts" such as "how he'd learn to walk on crutches, briskly and smartly" and how he could now read all "the essential books he'd hitherto missed" instead of wasting evenings with other boys (391). Despite the element of rationalization here, we believe him, and admire him much as does Kostoglotov, who notices that he seems to have grown older as a result of his operation and its aftermath. Kostoglotov also notices that "he was interested in others" (390), a simple enough characteristic, perhaps even a cliché, but one which, like the words "good" and "evil," Solzhenitsyn wishes to reinvigorate whenever he can. Asya, however, can only groan over her misfortune: "What have I got to live for?" (393). Compared to Dyomka, she behaves badly—and Solzhenitsyn is unrelenting in making her a kind of seventeen-year-old monster of misplaced values. She is convinced that no man would want her now, that only fools love girls for their characters—although Dyomka, presumably not a fool but certainly without the glamor she expects in a male, offers to marry her. At the end of the scene, she bares her breast, the one about to be removed:

> "Listen to me, you'll be the last one! You're the last one who can see it and kiss it. No one but you will ever kiss it! Dyomka, *you* at least must kiss it, if nobody else!" (394)

He does. He nuzzles it "gratefully, admiringly. . . . Its beauty flooded him" (395).

Asya doesn't offer him her breast because she loves him but rather because she loves her breasts and this entire incident becomes a grotesque (and overdrawn) ritual meant to indicate the extent of her self-worship. After learning of the imminent loss of her breast, Asya could have changed for the better, but Solzhenitsyn does not allow it; he seems to take an almost perverse delight in giving her the fate she deserves. Certainly the complacency of handsome pleasure-seeking young materialists can be annoying, but the message of this incident, which is that the "life is for happiness" ideology leaves one totally unprepared for facing difficulties, is being shouted too loudly at the reader and is worked out too easily.

Obviously, Asya's answer to the central question of the novel, what do men live by, is unsatisfactory. But even though Dyomka suddenly becomes somewhat pathetic, too, taking what he can get for the first and perhaps last time in his life, Asya does do him the favor of teaching him genuine facts of the sort which neither Aunt Styofa nor anyone else could give him. And we leave the scene confident of his (earned and tested) moral superiority to Asya.

Shortly after Dyomka and Asya become acquainted (Chapter 10), there is a chapter devoted to Zoya, the beautiful medical student and nurse, who is interested in Kostoglotov. Only six years older than Asya but vastly more experienced in the hardships of this world, her attitudes toward sex and other human values are meant to be compared to Asya's. In addition, the Zoya-Kostoglotov relationship (along with the Vera-Kostoglotov relationship) provides Solzhenitsyn an opportunity to examine in some depth the impact that an attractive woman has on a mature man who has lived most of his adult life in an essentially womanless world. Like Asya, Zoya loves to dance, values her impressive breasts, has had "the overwhelming moments" (155) with a number of young men, and associates with girl friends who believe that "everything possible should be grabbed from life immediately and with both hands" (155). Unlike Asya, however, she knows the value of a good man (as opposed to a handsome one) and the value of continuity and stability in a relationship.

How did she gain this knowledge? Apart from the fact that she is more intelligent than Asya, she has a wise old proverb-uttering grandmother whom she respects and who gives her sound advice, which she sometimes takes. Zoya does not claim to know all the answers. More importantly for her education, she has childhood memories of the "hungry, tense life of the war years," the "long, frenzied evacuation of Smolensk" (155), and other events in which she came face to face with human suffering. There is much she doesn't know; for instance, Kostoglotov discovers that she, like most of the other staff members in the cancer ward, is woefully ignorant of the workings of the Gulag world. But her own suffering has taught her to respect those who have "been put to the test" (168), who have become stronger as a result of what they have endured. When Kostoglotov describes the fate of his former fiancée, Zoya notices that "he was capable of genuine feeling" (168), as if the very existence of genuine feeling is so rare that it is worth remarking over.

And as we know from other sources in Solzhenitsyn's work, he does believe genuine feeling to be rare, not because there is a law against it but because in so many ways his society teaches that it is a sign of weakness, especially among those who see themselves as purposeful revolutionaries building a new society. People everywhere who choose to be tough-minded realists usually keep themselves from yielding to any incipient deep feelings they may have; but Soviet society in particular sanctions hard-bitten attitudes, as Solzhenitsyn so eloquently explains in that section of *Gulag II* entitled "Our Muzzled Freedom" (632–655). And it may be that this sort of ideological toughness is actually a form of innocence. The ironically fortunate thing about those who have suffered or have deeply felt the suffering of others is that they cannot teach themselves *not* to feel; they are sensitive and alert in ways which others know nothing about. But for many progressive realists genuine feeling (like love or pity) would be distracting; it would make one pause; to recognize its authority would be to complicate human affairs, and dealing with complications is difficult. So without any practice in exercising their feelings, such people become increasingly callow. Most of the young boys Zoya knows wish only to "warm themselves up a bit, have their fun and then clear out" (155). They undoubtedly think themselves tough and strong, but in Zoya's eyes Kostoglotov's form of strength "was something she had never met before in the boys she went with" (168).

Once Kostoglotov has established himself as an extraordinary and sensitive man, beautiful Zoya is willing to help reinitiate him to the delights of sensuality. She flirts with him, parades and poses for him, sees herself as a gift to him, and feels a "surging compulsion to do as he asked" (164). For a man as sex-starved as he is, she is a dream come true, exactly what he needs at this point in his new life. What is important about the beginning of this relationship is that each person respects the experience of the other and finds the other worthy of his affection. Kostoglotov is full of lust ("All those wayward, tangled and conventional desires were returning to him" [169]), and Zoya is not without it, but before they consider yielding to it, they carefully assess one another's character. (Asya will ask Dyomka, "What sort of fool loves a girl for her character?" [394]). So for a moment Zoya and Kostoglotov seem to have gained the possibility of a flourishing relationship in which both sexuality and a kind of ethical compatibility are present. Some of the happiest lines in Solzhenitsyn are those where the two of them acknowledge the delight of their flirtation, the reciprocal "force" (170) between them, and the possibility of a future together.

Unfortunately, as happens so often in his work when a healthy romantic relationship between adults seems about to be established, Solzhenitsyn will not allow it to last. It is as if he fears to suggest what is so often true: Romantic love *can* be a source of profound happiness, a refuge from a larger world, and perhaps even a defensible reason for not doing one's duty in that larger world. He does not want to leave his readers with images of thoughtful people like Kostoglotov going off into the Kazakhstan sunset and living blissfully ever after. Romantic love and sex, while important, cannot be the primary aim of his heroes' lives. Just when Zoya and Kostoglotov seem to have reached an understanding and Zoya is basking in his "steady, absorbing admiration" (170), she makes a mistake, one that reminds us that despite her sensitivity she is, after all, only twenty-three. She begins to sing a popular song, "her whole body writhing." To make matters worse, the song is from the movie *The Tramp*, which romanticizes into Robin Hoods those prison camp thieves and cutthroats Solzhenitsyn emphatically condemns in Chapter 16 of *Gulag II*. Almost immediately she realizes her mistake, but it is too late. This reminder of prison, as well as her own misinformation regarding that institution, turns Kostoglotov into a sick man again. He is suddenly infected by bad memories: "He looked past her, a cruel expression on his face. His jaw tightened slightly. It was a disagreeable movement" (171). Their carefree interlude abruptly becomes an occasion for Kostoglotov to explain a few of the facts to Zoya. She is receptive to what he says; indeed, she looks at him "almost as if she felt guilty about something" (171), but it is clear that Kostoglotov's past and Zoya's youth grate against each other and would probably continue to do so in the future. One suspects that insofar as she is a contemporary young woman (she goes to the movies, listens to popular songs, etc.), she cannot even *exist* without giving him (and Solzhenitsyn behind him) cause to wince now and then.

However, when we next see them together (Chapter 18) they both recognize that the "gay multicolored wheel of their game had to roll a little further . . ." (233). They talk and feel like potential lovers. Zoya is seriously considering a life in exile with Kostoglotov; she holds neither his age nor his imprisonment against him. He in turn actually proposes marriage to her. But this time the problem Solzhenitsyn creates makes them puppets in his hands. The life-saving injections which Kostoglotov has been receiving, Zoya tells him, will also make him impotent, and we discover that she does not want that. So the issue becomes sex versus life, and Zoya's previous characterization as a woman with humane values is undercut. As Asya did, she becomes a much too convenient way for Solzhenitsyn to illustrate, as Helen Muchnic puts it, the "rapt selfishness of physical desire."[7] Although Kostoglotov is shocked by the news of his forthcoming impotence, at the moment he is preoccupied with lust. Their next move, as summarized by Muchnic, is this:

> For the sake of being alone with her, he helps her fill the oxygen balloon required by a man in the last stages of lung cancer. The task means nothing to them; the secluded corner where they are at work is a trysting place and while the balloon is being inflated, he clasps her passionately to himself and they forget all about it, barely managing to turn off the tap before it bursts.

Even then they only get to kiss each other. We are probably meant to be outraged by their indifference to the dying man, but we know that under ordinary circumstances Kostoglotov would *not* be indifferent. As is often the case when Solzhenitsyn wants it both ways, there is a two-toned narrative voice in this scene. One is heavy with character-killing moral censure: "Today might be the day he was going to die, Oleg's brother and neighbor, abandoned and hungry for sympathy" (242). The other voice, with which the chapter ends, reinforces one of the main themes of the novel, the reawakening of Kostoglotov to the small delights of life:

> He had forgotten what it was like, and so it was all the more unexpected to feel that aching sensation again, to feel lips crushed till they were rough and swollen with kisses. It made his whole body young (243).

160

Even with due allowances for irony, this is not condemnation. It is an expression of how much he has missed in the past and of how little he is asking for in the present. Kostoglotov's indifference to the dying man is deplored by Solzhenitsyn but also understood by him, and this final paragraph sounds very much like forgiveness.

In all his novels Solzhenitsyn puts his characters under the pressure of life-and-death situations. His best people never take life for granted (and never regard happiness as its end), rarely receive much material reward from it but are experts at appreciating what little they do receive—and, finally, usually after a considerable struggle, find themselves capable of sacrificing life or its pleasures entirely for the sake of principle, for the sake of doing what is right. When Kostoglotov and Zoya finally and mutually reject each other (Chapter 27), it is a milepost on Kostoglotov's road to even higher moral ground than he was on at the beginning of the novel (where he was merely cheerful, decent, stoical, and skeptical). Of course, Solzhenitsyn has by this time made it easy for him to reject Zoya, now a game-playing, unprincipled older version of Asya; she is dismissed with a few perfunctory lines. Earlier we learned that her very name meant "life," but she, too, eventually equates "life" with "sex," and Kostoglotov is on the road to learning that there is more to life than that. He does not *yet* want to learn it. He is still angry with Zoya for not yielding to him. He is still angry with Vera Gangart for prescribing the injections (as if right now he *would* rather have sex than be cured of cancer, an impulse just extravagant enough to be believed). But it is also Vera, sexually innocent herself, who will teach him some things he has never fully realized before.

The most interesting aspect of Kostoglotov and Vera's relationship, however, has little to do with the obvious lesson he receives from her, which is, as Muchnic puts it, this:

From the first, in appearance, manner, gestures, Vera has seemed to Kostoglotov an embodiment of light, grace, gentleness, and brightness. She revives his faith in something other than the reality of universal grossness that has been his lot, in the purity he has known in childhood and the beauty he has always found in art and nature.[8]

Both Oleg and Vera are over thirty, both are highly intelligent and sensitive, both have been exposed to pain and suffering, and both have had very few romantic or sexual encounters. This latter fact is unusual among people of their age and experience, and all their conversations are colored by a curious tint of almost adolescent uncertainty, misapprehension, mutual embarrassment, and awkwardness. Sometimes it is Solzhenitsyn himself who is awkward and embarrassing in presenting their points of view ("With a woman like that," he has Kostoglotov reflect, the leering ellipses his own, "one always wonders if she has yet . . ." [221]), but for the most part he renders well a situation in which the sexual and emotional innocence of two mature adults is plausible—and that is not easy to do. The walking-on-eggs quality of their relationship, their mutual hesitation to overcommit themselves, and their failure to get together at the end is perhaps frustrating to the reader (who wants some sort of consummation) but is also believably poignant. Each recognizes the other's merits, yet they treat each other so delicately that they are bound to make silly miscalculations. When Oleg goes to Vera's apartment house, it seems right that he is intimidated by the aggressive woman and the young man with the motorcycle (another of those pillars of insensitivity which Solzhenitsyn plants in his work). These small barriers are just enough to sap what little self-confidence he has been able to muster. But Solzhenitsyn loses credibility when he has Oleg write Vera a letter in which he rejects their potential future relationship on the grounds of principle (something "false and forced might have started between us" [529]). As I said before, the entire theme of his forthcoming impotence seems merely a melo-

162

dramatic device to raise the stakes a degree higher than they need be. Long before this moment we know that Oleg is a man of principle and high idealism. Regarding the ending, however, Helen Muchnic thinks quite differently than I do:

> Kostoglotov's decision is rational and magnanimous. It is a measure of his love and the crowning instance of the human ideal toward which the whole book has been directed, recalling all its discussions about the meaning of happiness and the purpose of life and all the dramatic examples of these. Kostoglotov himself in consenting at last to hormone therapy has already concluded that a man does not primarily live for sex. But to sacrifice another's happiness to his own inadequacy is another matter; and although it was Vera who has persuaded him, he cannot, in callous selfishness, take advantage of her generosity and inexperience; his conscience "forbids" him to see her again.[9]

In *The First Circle* a number of the Stalinist bureaucrats and administrators are secretly miserable and even capable of acknowledging twinges of guilty conscience for the evil which they help perpetuate. In *Cancer Ward* the principal Stalinist is Rusanov, a veteran personal records administrator, a man of limited intelligence and imagination who wants the best for himself and his family and has managed to receive just that from the regime which he enthusiastically supports. He loves his job and finds it interesting and exciting. He is probably the most obnoxious character in all of Solzhenitsyn's work. He is given a great deal of space in the novel, probably because Solzhenitsyn regards him as typical of thousands of very ordinary men and women who are devoted to the system and help make it work. How can they be so devoted? Rusanov is one answer to that question, a constant one in Solzhenitsyn's work.

Rusanov is not a loyal Party man because he has

thought about it. Despite his continuous mouthing of the ideologically correct slogans, even other Communists like Vadim notice that he states them "as if he had learned them by heart" (252). He is loyal because he is comfortable and rather stupid, a sleek fat frog perched on a lily pad. From the very beginning his complacency, self-importance, and materialism are rendered so well that one of the main elements of suspense in *Cancer Ward* is whether he will receive his just reward. In a sense, he does—he has terminal cancer. Unfortunately, he is too imperceptive to realize that himself; he is released from the hospital thinking he is cured, and so never experiences the agonies of realization which we uncharitably wish upon him. Occasionally it looks as if the suffering caused by his tumor or his memory of past evil deeds *will* have a positive effect on him; at one point we learn that "for five weeks the tumor had dragged him along like a fish on a hook, and he had become kinder, or perhaps simpler" (372), and at another we witness his own self-assessment: "He knew he had no outstanding qualities except devotion to duty, thoroughness, and perseverance . . ." (278), but the last time we see him, being chauffeured away from the clinic by his automobile-worshipping younger children, they nearly run down Kostoglotov, about whom Rusanov grumbles, "He's a class enemy" (463).

That line alone tells us that, despite several opportunities, he has learned nothing of value from his experience at the cancer ward. Although many have tried, no one has been able to shock this man into questioning the dozen or so canned responses that he has available for practically every contingency of life. As we have seen elsewhere in Solzhenitsyn, a person's intelligence is often measured by the extent to which he *can* be enlightened by harrowing experiences—and the most direct evidence of this change is that the language he subsequently uses seems fresh and clean, as if washed. Solzhenitsyn's work is full of people who unexpectedly undergo such a change. Rusanov, however, is the most fully developed example of another group of people whose active intelligence is limited, and when these people are also without spiritual or moral supports of any kind, a readily available, nationally accepted, authoritative-sounding jargon is hardly something that imprisons them. On the contrary, it gives them identity, security, and a sense of freedom. Rusanov can be temporarily hurt by the insults hurled at him by smarter men like Kostoglotov (who calls him, among other things, a son-of-a-bitch and a racist), but in the end his orthodoxy is like protective armor, and he is invulnerable—which is absolutely maddening to Kostoglotov, who loses his own temper more than once in Rusanov's presence. In Rusanov there is no active intelligence or conscience to which one *can* make an appeal.

During what is probably meant to be the most significant dialogue in the novel, Shulubin asks Kostoglotov:

> "But how many are they, these people who believed, the ones who didn't understand? I know you can't expect much from a young boy, but I just cannot accept that our whole people suddenly became weak in the head. I can't believe it, I won't! In the old days the lord of the manor stood on the porch of his mansion and talked a lot of nonsense, but the peasants only smirked quietly into their beards. The lord of the manor saw them, so did the bailiffs standing on his side. And when the time came to bow down, true, they all bowed 'as one man.' But does that mean peasants believed the lord of the manor? What sort of person do you have to be to believe?" (434)

My answer would be: You have to be like Rusanov. A bit further on, Shulubin gives his answer, which is familiar to readers of Solzhenitsyn: "The people are intelligent enough, it's simply that they wanted to live" (434). But not all people *are* intelligent enough, and while, as Shulubin himself would say, there can't "really be a whole nation of fools" (434), there can certainly be a lot of fools in the nation. Rusanov is one of them, and unfortunately he is in a position of power. There are times when Solzhenitsyn casts about for grandiose cultural formulations, as if there really may be a monolithic entity called the Russian people about which it is safe to generalize, but his greater strength is as a subdivider of his world into character types (and sometimes even further into unique individuals). The portrait of Rusanov is a more credible answer to Shulubin's question than anything else in the novel, even though Solzhenitsyn himself does not seem fully to realize this.

Rusanov's job is based on taking full advantage of the fact that something "negative or suspicious can always be noted down against any man alive. Everyone is guilty of something or has something to conceal" (189). During Solzhenitsyn's detailed description of that job (188–194) it becomes clear that men like Rusanov find intimidating others from a comfortable behind-the-scenes position profoundly exciting. It amounts to fun.

> Rusanov's mysterious, isolated, almost supernatural position in the general production system gave him a satisfyingly deep knowledge of the true processes of life. The life familiar to everybody—work, conferences, factory newssheets, local trade-union announcements pinned up at the checkpoint, applications for various benefits, the cafeteria and the factory club—was not real, it only seemed so to the uninitiated. The acual direction life took was decided without loud publicity, calmly, in quiet offices, by two or three people who understood one another, or by dulcet telephone calls. The stream of real life ran on in the secret papers that lay deep in the briefcases of Rusanov and his colleagues. For years this life might follow a man in silence, then suddenly and momentarily it would reveal itself, breathing fire from its jaws as it rose from its underground kingdom, wrenching off a victim's head or belching fire over him, then disappearing, no one knew where. Afterward everything remained the same on the surface—club, cafeteria, applications for benefits, newssheets, work—yet as the workers walked past the factory checkpoint one man

would be missing—dismissed, removed or eliminated (192).

People considerably more intelligent and sensitive than Rusanov often wish to think themselves privy to "the true processes of life." And it can be fascinating to find oneself in a situation where one can "manipulate the threads" (189) of other people's lives, to watch how they respond to the tone of voice in which one says good morning, to watch them squirm with discomfort in one's presence. But most people do resist the enchantment of this sort of evil. They have reasons for resisting it. Rusanov's only fear (short of dying) is "simply of being beaten up" (185). Kostoglotov is not about to beat him up. The best he can do is offer tough-guy responses, as, for instance, when Rusanov complainingly inquires why Kostoglotov must have the light left on and Kostoglotov answers, "So I can pick my asshole" (20). Except in moral and spiritual terms, men like Rusanov are far more than a match for the Kostoglotovs and the Shulubins, and Solzhenitsyn knows it.

Characteristically, however, he leaves us with a sliver of hope even within the portrait of the worst man in his fiction. One of Rusanov's sons, Yuri, a new member of a legal inspection team, has a dawning sense that his father's total dedication to the state and its laws is really a dedication to the delightful process of administering rules and regulations and has nothing to do with seeking justice for individual human beings. Yuri himself is hardly a potential rebel, but he has a conscience (his father finds him "weak and flabby in most things" [398]); after his first inspection tour he is capable of wondering whether "there was any point in his work at all" (402). Yuri has allowed himself to become personally involved in individual cases, to look closely at the motivations and circumstances of those who have violated the "law," and for this his father scolds him. The last time we see Yuri, he is somewhat bewildered, but at least he knows that life is far more complicated than his father ever perceived it.

167

Although Rusanov is the most fully developed bad man in *Cancer Ward*, a man whose smugness and predictability stand as a concrete marker against which all other sensibilities can be measured, there are many other individuals whose attitudes irritate the thinkers, Kostoglotov and Shulubin, both of whom are easily exasperated. Indeed, one of the novel's distinguishing features is that so many of its less admirable characters present themselves with guileless certainty, and their attitudes are like sharpened spikes to those good, truth-seeking, idealistically inclined characters who, in the end, we are asked to regard as Russia's hope. When Kostoglotov returns to his place of exile it is as if he has made a separate peace (though not an irresponsible one, as we shall see), removing himself at least for the time being from a crowded cancer ward and city where he had learned that most people are indifferent to this vision of truth—even though he *has* had unexpected success in gaining an audience for his views. There is the geologist Vadim who, much to the disgust of Kostoglotov and Shulubin, believes that science and ethics should be separate and who justifies his (brief) life's work on the ground that it is "interesting" (378); there is the irresponsible Chaly, openly and joyfully dedicated to being an operator, who proclaims that "we only live once, so why not live well" (319), who leaves Shulubin staring, virtually wordless; there is the former prison guard Ahmadjan, who says of the men he guarded, "They no human beings! They no human beings!" (458) and who justifies his work by declaring, "Those up top—not my business. I swear oath—I serve. They force you—you serve. . . ." (459); and there is Kostoglotov's surprised discovery that upon Stalin's death two years before "old men had shed tears, young girls had wept" in the outside world, whereas in prison hundreds of men grinned, felt triumphant, and "threw their caps in the air!" (315) Because, as Kostoglotov notes of Ahmadjan, those knotty attitudes are "sincere and straightforward" (458), nothing Kostoglotov can say or do has much effect on them. Moreover, Solzhenitsyn sees to it that Vadim and Chaly have somewhat more to them than a one-dimensional arrogant devotion to science and life-force respectively. Even if Shulubin were in a position to demand that the entire Soviet Union adopt what he calls "ethical socialism" (441), the ordinary attitudes of ordinary people like these would stand in the way.

Shulubin's conversation with Kostoglotov in Chapter 31 ("Idols of the Market Place") is, as Helen Muchnic has said, "a recapitulation of the cardinal points at issue in the novel: the nature of truth, the place of the individual in Soviet society, the meaning of happiness, the value of life, the tragedy of guilt."[10] Victor Erlich finds it interesting that "it is the guilt-ridden ex-conformist Shulubin who is entrusted with articulating as positive a moral-political vision as any found in the Solzhenitsyn *oeuvre*—a vision of 'ethical socialism'. . . ."[11] In Shulubin's own words, "We have to show the world a society in which all relationships, fundamental principles and laws flow directly from ethics, and from them *alone*" (442). There is no question that Solzhenitsyn wants us to take Shulubin very seriously. His discussion with Kostoglotov comes at a strategic point late in the novel when, yes, it is helpful to have the larger issues clarified in the midst of all the detail and individual portraits. And since Kostoglotov himself has up to this point been the novel's most reliable source of wisdom, common sense, and hope as well as of outrage and indignation—all garnered by his close observation of experience, of trusting to what he sees rather than what he hears—it is fitting that he encounter this formally educated former professor, who in some respects has more knowledge than Kostoglotov—and not just conceptual knowledge, either. Shulubin has been a book-burner and a cowardly retreater into the quiet haven of "pure biology" (437–438); his children have betrayed him; he is full of self-loathing for being one of the millions who remained silent when men like Rusanov worked their wills; he is a champion sufferer, a wise man, a skillful theorist; he has rectal cancer; he suspects that the soul is immortal. In fact, Solzhenitsyn stuffs him with more significance than he can bear, and I have some reservations about him.

Shulubin speaks with authority when he names what went wrong with Soviet society and why—he has much hard *information* that is unavailable to Kostoglotov's common sense and wide-open eyes—but when he begins to expound on his notion of ethical socialism, of how society ought to be, he begins to speak "very distinctly, like a master giving a lesson" (442), and Kostoglotov begins to wither a little under the rapid-fire certainty of his talk. "Ethical demands," he tells Kostoglotov,

"must determine all considerations: how to bring up children, what to train them for, to what end the work of grownups should be directed, and how their leisure should be occupied. As for scientific research, it should only be conducted where it doesn't damage morality, in the first instance where it doesn't damage the researchers themselves. The same should apply to foreign policy" (442).

We know that Solzhenitsyn supports many of Shulubin's ideas, yet we also know that Solzhenitsyn distrusts intellectualism. There is in the above passage a hint of that ominous tone of a man who has a program, who sounds as if he has anticipated in advance all possible objections to his theories, and who as the conversation continues (with Kostoglotov making half-hearted objections now and then) begins to shine "with the excitement of an animal about to overtake its quarry" (443).

"So you see," he said, "that's what ethical socialism is. One should never direct people toward happiness, because happiness too is an idol of the market place. One should direct them toward mutual affection. A beast gnawing at its prey can be happy too, but only human beings can feel affection for each other, and this is the highest achievement they can aspire to" (443).

There is good sense here but also that impulse of intellectuals to want to "direct" people toward this or that ostensible good. Moreover, the phrase "ethical socialism" has even in this brief conversation begun to sound like jargon and is a concept which could easily spawn a new set of those pat "phrases and formulas which do violence to reason" that Shulubin himself earlier condemned (436). When Kostoglotov puts in a good word for "happiness," the tormented Shulubin asserts that happiness is a "mirage" and continues to lecture on the subject until he begins to feel ill. Certainly Solzhenitsyn supports Shulubin's opinion that the State's dedication to the so-called "happiness of future generations" is presumptuous (no one "should have the effrontery to try to plan it in advance" [443]), and certainly the "mutual affection" which Shulubin recommends is a somewhat less nebulous concept than "happiness," but Shulubin himself is a brooder, a dour judge of others, a man who shows little affection for anyone until Kostoglotov makes an overture in his direction. His idealism is dogmatic and a subject mostly for discussion, and his program seems somewhat removed from the realm of possibility. Actually, Shulubin's most impressive moment is just before his death:

"There's a fragment, isn't there? . . . Just a tiny fragment," he kept whispering.
It was then it struck Oleg that Shulubin was not delirious, that he'd recognized him and was reminding him of their last conversation before the operation. He had said, "Sometimes I feel quite distinctly that what is inside of me is not all of me. There's something else, sublime, quite indestructible, some tiny fragment of the universal spirit. Don't you feel that?" (483)

Here he whispers, questions, hopes, suspects—but does not lecture. He suddenly has the authority of a dying man. Moreover, this educated intellectual has here the same perceptions as the ignorant worker Yefrem Poddevyev had earlier, thus making them equal in the end— or rather the beginning.

171

Nowhere in Solzhenitsyn's work does he seriously offer the hope that eventually, somehow, mankind will find itself immersed in a sweet-scented bath of mutual affection. He is acutely aware of our potential for evil and of the actual evils of everyday life. But even though the societies in all of his novels are in a sorry condition, the origin of which he goes to great lengths to explain, that condition need not be as bad as it is. How does one make it better? As I see it, part of the purpose of *Cancer Ward*, once the evil people have been named and seen clearly, is to show how another group of people, for a number of different reasons, practice individual acts of goodness in their daily lives, and, whenever they can, resist those forms of violence which fall into their paths. It is as if he is saying to his (virtually nonexistent) Soviet readers, "Look to these characters of mine for examples of attainable virtue." As he says in the Nobel Lecture, we "must not reconcile ourselves to being defenseless and disarmed; we must not sink into a heedless, feckless life—but go out to the field of battle" (38). In Solzhenitsyn's fiction (except for *August 1914*) that battlefield is close to home; Aunt Styofa, Vera Gangart, Lev Leonidovich, Dr. Oreshchenkov, the Kadmins (one of the few happy couples in Solzhenitsyn), Dyomka, and many minor characters all find small ways to fight that battle. And throughout the novel Kostoglotov is the battler we know best.

By the end a part of him simply has had enough, does not want to fight any more, wants only to live fully, wants happiness (despite all the beatings this concept takes). When he is released from the ward this part of him responds to the world as if it is "the morning of creation" (485); he walks through the "Old Town" in a state of childlike wonder, receptive to what it can teach him, acutely aware of simple, sensory delights, of unhurried pleasures, of lives based on ancient rhythms. For a few pages, in one of the great rebirth scenes in literature, we see how Kostoglotov's years of suffering and deprivation have so honed his sensitivity that the smallest events and objects become exquisitely interesting and press in upon him with almost threatening clarity. It is a fine interlude, a testimony to the riches available in common life to an alerted and appreciative sensibility. Solzhenitsyn could end the novel on this note and we would probably not be disappointed.

But Kostoglotov's moral vision likewise is sensitive and sharp. As his first day of creation wears on, his initial enchantment with everything he sees under the bright sunshine is muted by the moral implications of other things he sees. He is, for instance, sickened by the disparity between the materialism he discovers in the department store and his awareness that there "were men rotting in the trenches, men being thrown into mass graves, into shallow pits in the perma frost, men being taken into camps for the first, second and third times; men being jolted from station to station in prison trucks, wearing themselves out with picks, slaving away to be able to buy a patched-up quilt jacket . . ." (498). Solzhenitsyn, unfortunately, belabors the effect of the department store on Kostoglotov, and then, during the zoo scene, besieges us with tortured analogies between the condition of men and the condition of animals, but it *is* fitting that Kostoglotov will not be so caught up in its delights that he will forget "who are the guilty ones of this world" (507).

Kostoglotov's responses to two events near the end reveal the scale of the hope which *Cancer Ward* offers. When he goes to get his papers cleared before leaving the city, he encounters a kind N.K.V.D. official:

> Oleg was genuinely moved; there was even a tightness in his throat. How little was needed. But a few humane men behind these vile desks and life became completely different (518).

Although the man's kindness may represent only a temporary change in N.K.V.D. policy, it is exactly this sort of small action which, when multiplied, sets a tone for an entire society, a tone which Solzhenitsyn sees as having been missing for years. As bland as it is to say, wouldn't it be nice if people always acted like this, no matter what the official policy and who was in control of the state? Earlier, as Kostoglotov was telling the ward about Dr. Maslennikov, who writes ten letters a day to patients across the country, he exclaimed, "he doesn't have to do it, it's not his job, he just does it as a good deed" (139). We know that such small actions, which seem to be within everyone's power, can make life better for everyone. And we also know how difficult it is in one's hour-by-hour life to move outside of oneself and make kindness a habit (which is not far, I realize, from Shulubin's doctrine of mutual affection). If the N.K.V.D. official and others like him became genuinely interested in the personal problems of the Kostoglotovs, then we would have the beginnings of a benevolent bureaucracy which heretofore has been only a dream in Solzhenitsyn's works. Solzhenitsyn does not suggest that this is about to occur universally. He wants merely in this incident to show, as if his readers can never receive the lesson too often, the power of common decency.

The other important incident near the end of *Cancer Ward* is when Kostoglotov intimidates a loudmouth who is trying to crowd into line at the train station; the "ignorant eye might have taken him for a psychopath and let him go to the front of the line, but Oleg at once recognized him as a self-styled camp hoodlum. He was trying to frighten people, as his sort always does" (530). Kostoglotov does not let the man have his way. It takes courage to interfere with this kind of very ordinary incivility. Most people would let it go by. But Kostoglotov "wanted things done honestly and in the proper way" (530), and this incident signals to us that he will try to defend honesty and propriety when he can, which is more than most people do. The danger that could easily lie in wait for a former prisoner, cancer patient, and man-in-exile is to think that he has done enough, suffered enough, and now deserves to be free from moral responsibility. That will not happen to Kostoglotov. It did not happen to Solzhenitsyn.

CHAPTER FOUR

August 1914

Part of an even longer work-in-progress, *August 1914* is Solzhenitsyn's most ambitious and impressive novel to date. For readers coming to it after the others, it succeeds in ways that may be surprising. In addition to Solzhenitsyn's usual moral and philosophical themes and his search for an answer to the question of how twentieth-century Russia went wrong, much of *August 1914* reads like an adventure story. It is full of action, guns and blood, heroism and cowardice, advances and retreats, and often the faint hope, even though the reader knows better, that everything may work out in the end. Which of the generals will succeed? Who among our favorite characters will get out of this alive? Can Colonel Vorotýntsev do any good? When will the roof fall in? It is not to underrate Solzhenitsyn's achievement or the significance of his subject to say that he keeps the multiple plots taut, keeps us wondering what will happen next, and gives us an enormous fund of nuts-and-bolts information about the war.

One distinguished critic says that the military logistics are "bewildering to anybody but a military specialist"; another claims that the novel is weighed down with "operational detail."[1] But in my opinion the great strength of *August 1914* is that its technical detail is made interesting and accessible, released gradually, and eventually educates the reader with remarkable precision. Once we accustom ourselves to consulting a map and pausing now and then to regain our bearings, it is satisfying to observe Solzhenitsyn's clarity about the complicated Battle of Tannenberg. He knows the terrain and the actors even better than he has to.[2] And in spite of the frequency of Colonel Vorotýntsev's back-and-forth movements and the many chapter-to-chapter changes of scene in the center of the novel, all of which give the impression of furious activity, Solzhenitsyn has his material well under control. *August 1914* is partly *about* confusion and disorder, as is any novel which truly makes war its subject, but it is not confused or disordered itself.

Solzhenitsyn's subject allows him a new kind of authorial freedom and makes for an out-in-the-open atmosphere. In the relatively confined space of the prisons and the cancer ward, where the possibilities for physical action and changes of scene were limited, he often had to labor to keep the narrative moving. *The First Circle* and *Cancer Ward* are full of talk, and when the pace slackens, new characters are introduced, bearing with them matter for even more talk. In all three earlier novels there are more "issues" than in *August 1914*, where we are required to pay careful attention but are not so consistently invited to be silent participants in moral and philosophical discussions. *August 1914* has more views and vistas and is more panoramic; people move through the countryside, into towns and villages, over different kinds of landscapes. The novel begins:

They left the village on a clear morning at dawn. In

176

the early sunlight the whole of the Caucasus range, each single indentation, could be seen, brilliantly white with deep blue hollows, apparently so close at hand that a stranger to the region might have thought it a mere two hours' drive away.[3]

When we reach the war section (beginning at Chapter 10) we have more such passages: rich descriptions of the scene, the promise of some forthcoming event, the rhetoric of the story-teller. Solzhenitsyn does this sort of thing far better than we might have expected.

The first nine chapters are set primarily in a remote section of the southern Caucasus, but even here echoes of the beginning of the war are heard. The young Tolstoyan student, Sanya Lazhenitsyn, is about to enlist in the army for the simple reason that he feels "sorry for Russia" (10), a reason which angers his intellectual friends. (In a flashback to four years before, Sanya travels north to meet and have a brief chat with Tolstoy.) After Sanya, we are introduced to Irina Tomchak and the Tomchak family and see the way of life on their vast and flourishing estate. Among his many other activities, old Zakhar Tomchak is trying to arrange a draft exemption for his son Roman. Chapter 7 consists of a random selection of newspaper headlines, an always interesting if sometimes awkward device which Solzhenitsyn uses twice more in the novel. By the time we turn to the war in Chapter 10, we are anticipating future appearances of the dynamic Tomchak clan (which in fact does not happen in *August 1914* but surely will in future volumes).

In Chapter 10 Solzhenitsyn deftly describes Ostrolenka, brings the military situation up to date, introduces General Samsonov, the commander of the Second Army, shows the various pressures upon this good but indecisive man, and builds suspense. Colonel Vorotýntsev appears. He is a staff officer sent from General Headquarters to gather reliable information, but he also is thirsting for action: "The obsession which throbbed within him was to

177

solve a *riddle*; his destiny was to make a *decision*. . . ."
(115). Vorotýntsev is the principal character in *August
1914*. He sees what has gone wrong within the military
establishment and, if he had the power, he could set it
right; he is intelligent, kind, hard-working, effective. In
a sense he is the man we have been waiting for in Solzhenitsyn's work. After befriending Samsonov, Vorotýntsev travels on horseback to Soldau as the general's
representative and meets Colonel Krymov, a competent
officer like himself with whom he can speak candidly.
During their conversation, however, both men show small
but annoying faults—which is usually true of Solzhenitsyn's portraits of men he admires.

Meanwhile, we meet Second Lieutenant Yarik Kharitonov, newly graduated from the Alexandrovsky Military
Academy. Yarik is the oldest son of Aglaida Kharitonova,
the headmistress of the private girls' school in Rostov
where Zakhar Tomchak's daughter Xenya was educated.
(Similar connections between the civilians and the soldiers
are made throughout *August 1914*.) At home, Yarik had
been taught to live for "the good of the peasants" but he
had never actually seen any (144); now he commands a
platoon of them. We meet other members of his battalion,
including the "permanently dejected, whining" Second
Lieutenant Kozieko (151). Ensign Lenartovich, a young
revolutionary, and Fedonin, a dedicated army doctor,
discuss the merits of the war. All of these characters will
reappear later on.

Back in Ostrolenka, General Samsonov is trying to
conduct the war while beset by distractions, particularly
the incessant questions of the visiting English General
Alfred Knox (who in real life attributed the Russian defeat partly to the "low mental development" of the
Russian people[4]). In the next few chapters we meet
some excellent soldiers—Sergeant-Major Chernega, Captain Raitsev-Yartsev, Colonel Smyslovsky, Major-General
Nechvolodov—who demonstrate how effective the front-
line army can be when it is not interfered with by incompetent higher-ups. Chapter 23, subtitled "General

Situation up to August 13," is a wider view of the Eastern Front and a type of historical essay, one effect of which is to make us see the difference between history as conventionally written and historical fiction (there are three other chapters like it in the novel). Chapter 24 is about the energetic German General von François, and Chapter 25 is about the worst of the Russian Generals, Artamonov, whom Colonel Vorotýntsev is trying to help. Unlike Samsonov, General Artamonov does not recognize competence when he sees it and therefore regards Vorotýntsev as a spy and a leech.

At Usdau, Vorotýntsev finds himself in the trenches under fire with the men of the Vyborg regiment. Here he meets Arsenii Blagodaryov, a hearty and courageous private who becomes his loyal orderly. Vorotýntsev is part of a successful Russian initiative, a "spontaneous movement at company level," an example of the "immeasurable strength latent in the Russian people . . ." (304). In this section of *August 1914* are many scenes showing the characteristics of good officers (like Colonel Pervushin and General Martos) as opposed to poor ones (like General Klyuev). General Artamonov is the principal betrayer of Samsonov's plans (such as they are), and according to Colonel Krymov is "a fool, a coward, and a liar" (340). At one point we again meet Yarik Kharitonov, now struggling to reconcile the fact that the good peasant soldiers he so much admires also wish to loot a German village. Shortly afterwards he is wounded and sent to a hospital, where Colonel Vorotýntsev happens to meet him and admires his devotion to duty. Ensign Lenartovich also appears again, this time fleeing from battle on the grounds "that he was doing the wrong thing in the wrong place and that this was no place for him to die" (385). Meanwhile, General Samsonov is breaking down. The great retreat has begun, and there are several powerful scenes where common soldiers, many of them reservists who know nothing about politics or war, nevertheless stand and fight, drawing "on some unknown source of strength to cross the barrier that divides a man's love

179

of family and instinct of self-preservation from devotion to cruel duty" (446). Chapter 42 returns us to Moscow, where Sanya and a friend are making a farewell tour of the city. They meet and have a discussion about life with Varsonofiev, a philosopher and historian.

Back at the front, the collapse continues—along with intermittent acts of self-sacrifice and bravery, such as Sergeant-Major Chernega's orchestration of an artillery defense for retreating infantry. In the middle of the chaos, after doing as much as he can, Colonel Vorotýntsev is suddenly alone with his orderly Arsenii and, like most of the Russian army, encircled by the enemy. Yarik Kharitonov wanders on the scene—and together the men plan how to get away. (Vorotýntsev perceives it as his duty to return to the General Staff and tell the truth of what happened at Tannenberg.) As they move toward Russia, they pick up stragglers, including Ensign Lenartovich and some survivors of the Dorogobuzh regiment who have been carrying their wounded officer on their shoulders for twenty-five miles. During the journey of Vorotýntsev's little group and in the face of extreme danger and hardship, the characters of Yarik and Ensign Lenartovich as well as their attitudes toward the "people" are further developed by Solzhenitsyn. Major-General Nechvolodov appears again; he has carefully prepared his troops for a significant attack which could break the German encirclement of the army, but at the last minute he is ordered to retreat by his superiors, themselves far from the scene. Other characters reappear, including the beaten, suicidal, and pathetic Samsonov and the still-fighting Colonel Pervushin, a masterful leader who has such an affinity with his troops that "he never led them into an attack that was beyond their powers—but if he had, they would have followed him" (569).

Chapters 57 through 62 are about the home front. We learn of Ensign Lenartovich's family background and of his beautiful sister, Veronika. Ensign Lenartovich was taught to measure "people, events, and books by one yardstick: did they contribute to the emancipation of the people or to the consolidation of the state?" (618) We receive a glimpse of the intellectual environment at a college. We learn more about the Kharitonov household. We meet the brilliant engineer Obodovsky and the builder Arkhangorodsky. From these home-front chapters we are obviously intended to draw conclusions about further (non-military) causes of the future revolution.

The final two chapters examine the character of the basically good Grand Duke Nikolai Nikolaevich, show the influences upon him, implicitly criticize his irresponsible adoration of the Tsar and his own blind religiosity, and reveal the dismal ineptitude of his top aides. Chief-of-Staff Yanushkevich is a "small man with a puffy face, an insinuating manner, and a deep affection for paper and files" (700); Quartermaster General Danilov has a reputation for being Russia's top military strategist, but the "truth was that his forehead was solid bone, his mind moved at a snail's pace, and the thoughts which passed through it were worthless" (699). Vorotýntsev reports first to the Grand Duke and then, in one of the most abrasive scenes in Solzhenitsyn's works, to the assembled generals, whom he accuses of incompetence. General Zhilinsky is his special target. In the end Colonel Vorotýntsev is asked to leave the conference for having overstepped "the bounds of what is permissible" (713). The novel ends with news of the "colossal victory" at Lvov.

For those who have read the three earlier novels, Sanya's brief chat with Tolstoy near the beginning of *August 1914* is as amusing as it is significant. "Tell me if I have understood you rightly," says Sanya. "What is the aim of man's life on earth?" (17) It is among the important questions in Solzhenitsyn's work, one which he continually poses, and by now we are used to being referred to Tolstoy for an answer. But suddenly, early in *August 1914*, here we are face to face with "the gray-headed, gray-bearded Sage himself" (16) and another lengthy disquisition on the question seems imminent. Instead, Tolstoy answers succinctly, "To serve good and thereby to build the Kingdom of Heaven on earth" (17). Although scarcely confident about building heaven's kingdom on earth, all of Solzhenitsyn's heroes try in their way to serve good, but we see that that is easier said than done. As if a surrogate for the reader, Sanya, too, recognizes the difficulty: "But tell me, how do I serve good? Through love? Does it have to be through love?" (17) Tolstoy replies decisively, "Of course. Only through love." As any perceptive and intellectually inclined young man would, Sanya recognizes further complications:

> "Lev Nikolaevich," he said, "are you sure you're not exaggerating the power of love inherent in man, or at least in modern man? What if love isn't as strong as that, isn't necessarily to be found in everyone and may not prevail? Then your teaching would prove to be . . . fruitless, wouldn't it? Or very, very premature. Shouldn't one envisage a kind of intermediate stage with some less exacting demand and use *that* to awaken people to the need for universal good will? And then, after that, through love?" Before Tolstoy had time to answer, he added: "Because, as far as I can see, where we are in the South there simply *isn't* any universal good will, Lev Nikolaevich, none at all!" (18)

After all the evil enumerated in *Ivan Denisovich, The First Circle*, and *Cancer Ward*, it is as if Solzhenitsyn himself is, through Sanya, rechecking with one of the figures whom he reveres (despite substantial disagreements with him, as *August 1914* shows more clearly than any other work[5]). Although it is implied that Tolstoy could, if he wished, give a more elaborate answer, he merely repeats "without a moment's hesitation in words tested and matured by a lifetime: 'Only through love! Nothing else. No one will ever discover anything better' " (18).

Regarding a novel about carnage, catastrophe, and evil, in which one of the major points is the Russian army's unreadiness for modern warfare, it is possible to say that

Tolstoy's "tested and matured" words are deliberately placed early in the story only to have them rendered obsolete by subsequent events. But Solzhenitsyn wishes, in the most straightforward way he can, to reassert the primacy of love *before* he embarks on a narrative in which that value is easily obscured by the smoke of the battlefield. On a large scale, love does not prevail in *August 1914* any more than it does in other Solzhenitsyn works; it is seen only in those innumerable small exchanges of goodness between one person and another which he tucks into his fiction whenever he can. But as an ultimate value for men to hold it is nevertheless vastly superior to any other, particularly to the single-minded pursuit of pleasure or happiness. Putting it somewhat differently, Kathryn B. Feuer, in an excellent essay on Solzhenitsyn and Tolstoy, observes that whole group of characters in *August 1914*, including Sanya, Vorotýntsev, Irina Tomchak, Samsonov, even Grand Duke Nikolai Nikolaevich himself,

> are linked by love of God, love of country and love of their neighbor; indeed they are the true existence of the love which Tolstoy told Sania was the only means [to serve good and create the kingdom of heaven on earth.] They were Russia's hope who might have built—if not God's Kingdom on earth—at least a decent commonwealth in her territory, and it is their defeat which Solzhenitsyn depicts when Samsonov shoots himself.[6]

When Sanya hesitatingly asks the Sage if he is not "exaggerating the power of love inherent in man" he sounds sensible—what is more obvious than that the world is not governed by love? Just as the Bolsheviks later would talk about the intermediate steps along the road toward a pure Communist state, so Sanya, recognizing the absence of "universal good will," wishes to suggest that some "intermediate stage with some less exacting demand" be used to awaken people. But Tolstoy will have none of it. He is uncompromising in defending the ideal of love, and so is

Solzhenitsyn. To complicate this simple ideal by interjecting some preliminary or intermediate stage may appear intelligent, but it only leads to an attitude of mind which, while devoted to high ends, sanctions less than high means. When Tolstoy is first seen by Sanya walking through the trees "sometimes his head disappeared into the dense early-morning shadows; sometimes it was in sunshine, and at moments the light shining on the crown of his peaked linen cap seemed to surround his head with a halo" (16). On the subject of love, Tolstoy's head is in the sunshine and his saintliness in this respect is not intended as ironically inappropriate to the main business of the novel.

Among the most telling lines in the first nine chapters of *August 1914* are Zakhar Tomchak's reflections on the war:

> Now that the lush and prosperous years had started to come to Russia, the last thing she needed was a war; they should have just said a Requiem Mass for that Archduke Franz Ferdinand, after which the three emperors of Germany, Austria, and Russia should have drunk a glass of vodka at the wake and forgotten the whole affair (72).

In the picture Solzhenitsyn has given so far of the years immediately preceding the revolution there is no reason to think that he disagrees with Tomchak. In some rural areas things *are* getting better. Despite all the bluster, vulgarity, extravagance, and cunning in his personality, the elder Tomchak is a self-made man who has taken advantage of the latest advances in agricultural technology and is an efficient manager (particularly when compared to the generals, who, until now, have for some time had little to do except negotiate their way through the military bureaucracy). Although enormously rich, Tomchak is not evil. He respects his workers, and they respect him. We receive no indication that he oppresses anyone (except his wife, who discounts it, and his son Roman, who deserves it), and if we had expected to see a rural landscape in which cruel landowners are whipping emaciated workers into extracting what they can from the barren soil, then we are disappointed:

> In his office, too, Zakhar Tomchak never spent much time bent over rows of figures or piles of cash; he stayed there no longer than was necessary to make some decision. The real heart of his business was out on the steppes, with the machines and the flocks of sheep, and in the farmyard—*there* was the place to manage and supervise.
>
> Tomchak himself never missed a chance to watch the departure by rail or long-distance road-haulage of a consignment of grain, wool, or meat from his estate. It was his greatest and never-failing pleasure to see with his own eyes all that bulk and weight of his own produce being sent out into the world. He would sometimes boast: "I feed the whole of Russia," and he liked it when others praised him for it (75–6).

Apart from his understandable vanity, it is difficult in this passage to find anything to hold against Tomchak. Even though given to ostentatious displays of wealth (his seven-and-a-half-thousand-ruble car, his fancy gloves, etc.) and capable of bribing and bullying people (he "understood instinctively that generous payment for services rendered always makes for good relations between people" [51]), he knows he is performing a useful service, and he is right.

His great failure is his spoiled son, who is cowardly, self-indulgent, and pleasure-seeking; Roman seems a much more appropriate target for would-be revolutionaries than his father. Roman's wife, Irina, is trying her best to be a Christian and good wife even though she knows her marriage was a mistake; while living in luxury she is not spoiled, and while secretly miserable she does not whine. Seventeen-year-old Xenya Tomchak regards herself as

185

progressive and like her brother is theoretically in sympathy with the people and so berates herself, unconvincingly, for partaking of her family's "sinfully luxurious kind of life" (33); actually, she wants to have fun and be up-to-date, and she is too unformed to realize the significance of anything. Old Zakhar's wife, Evdokia, is a blacksmith's daughter who was "unable to get used to the idea of sitting down at table like a lady in her lace shawl and waiting to be served" (27). She and Zakhar still like to sleep on their "tiled stove-couch built peasant-fashion" (75).

The important thing about Solzhenitsyn's portrait of the Tomchak family is that he makes it difficult for us to lump them all together as irresponsible exploiters of the people. That would be much too simple a formulation. Not only have the elder Tomchaks (as well as Irina's father) found it possible to rise in pre-Revolutionary Russia; they do not forget their origins. The Tomchak "economy," as it is called, is not a utopia; some of the family members have misplaced values; and other problems are latent in their situation, but their economy and others like it *are* substantial accomplishments which benefit more people than merely their owners. They do more good than harm. Unfortunately, their weaknesses are highly visible, especially to the intelligentsia, and their strengths are easily taken for granted. As a result of the war and fashionable new ideas, such economies will be destroyed just when they are beginning to flourish.[7]

Like Zakhar Tomchak, the prominent engineer Obodovsky is also enthusiastic about the prospects for Russia's immediate future. Late in the novel, during his visit with Ilya Isakovich Arkhangorodsy, a highly successful builder of grain elevators and steam and electric mills, Obodovsky proclaims, "The great thing is—we're out of the doldrums! The doldrums are over for Russia! And when the wind blows, we can even make up our leeway!" (656) Several times in *August 1914* the idea is voiced that all "educated society" has a moral duty to aid the cause of revolution, but Obodovsky has already been a revolutionary (back in 1905) who was pardoned under the 1912 political amnesty. He was no parlor revolutionary, either. And he has been around—to America, to Germany. He knows how other countries do things. Even now he does not refuse to consider the possibility of revolution (if the government "hinders the development of a country, then we might have to take power" [658]), but he is much more interested in creating than in destroying. Give us "ten years of peaceful development and you won't recognize Russian industry—or Russian agriculture, for that matter" (657). Despite incompetence in high places, he believes that men like himself can work wonders, *if* there is peace and *if*, Solzhenitsyn implies, the revolutionaries do not have their way.

During the dinner party at the Arkangordskys' the two young social revolutionaries, Naum and Sonya, are scornful of Obodovsky's notion that "the best brains and hands in the country" should concentrate on creating wealth and leave the methods of distributing that wealth to "the second-raters"; when "enough has been built and made," he says, "then even if distribution is less than perfect, no one will be left completely without his share." To that argument Naum and Sonya say things like, "Create! Tsarism is preventing you from doing even that!" (666) But according to the evidence of *August 1914*, men like Obodovsky, Tomchak, and Arkhangorodsky have *already* created a great deal, even under the Tsar, whereas the revolutionaries have failed to see the positive changes going on before their very eyes. It is as if *they*, not the engineers and businessmen, are wedded to outdated conceptions of Russian reality and have lost touch with the creative potential of the people they presume to champion. Most of the revolutionaries would agree with Ensign Lenartovich that in "the long-term view" the sufferings and devastation of a war are good things, for they bring "the day of reckoning nearer" (163). But *August 1914* suggests that neither the war nor a day of reckoning was necessary. The process of modernizing Russia had begun (except, tragically, in the army), and the implied prediction of the novel is that the forthcoming revolution will only set back the process.

That proposition is, of course, debatable. In fact, Solzhenitsyn's protestations notwithstanding, many people would still say that without the revolution and its subsequent programs the "prodigies of the Russian advance," to use Robert B. Heilbroner's phrase, would *never* have occurred.[8] Heilbroner is eloquent on what it takes for underdeveloped countries to modernize:

> For the objectives of economic development do not lie, like a military citadel, exposed to the thrust of a single daring campaign. On the contrary, the development assault is better likened to a long grueling march through a hostile hinterland. The real resistance to development comes not from the old regimes, which can be quickly overcome, but from the masses of the population who must be wrenched from their established ways, pushed, prodded, cajoled, or threatened into heroic efforts, and then systematically denied an increase in well-being so that capital can be amassed for future growth. This painful reorientation of a whole culture, judging by past experience, will be difficult or impossible to attain without measures of severity; and when we add the need to maintain a fervor of participation long beyond the first flush of spontaneous enthusiasm, the necessity for stringent limitations on political opposition and for forcible means of assuring economic cooperation seems virtually unavoidable (85–86).

Heilbroner calculates that the transformation takes thirty to fifty years. If we need a reasonable justification for the cruelties of the modern Soviet state, Heilbroner provides one (although he is speaking of "under-developed countries" in the contemporary sense of the phrase, not of Russia in particular):

> . . . when we seek to project the problems of socialism in the underdeveloped areas, we cannot sidestep the probability that intellectual stiflement, political repression, and

188

enforced social conformity will figure prominently among them. Let me be quite explicit that when the alternatives of such a disciplined existence are degradation, misery, and premature death, the exercise of sternness and indoctrination appears in a very different light from that of an arbitrary and capricious tyranny. Nonetheless, the exercise of these measures, however necessary to assure the success of the development effort, is likely to affect the future of the nations who must suffer them no less severely than the hated influence of imperialism affected their past. When we look to that future and inquire as to the outlook for socialism in the backward lands, it is necessary to recognize that it is likely to emerge both as the salvation of its otherwise doomed people, and also as the source of a moral and intellectual infection from which it may take generations to recover (86–87).

Solzhenitsyn's novels before *August 1914* demonstrate repeatedly that a moral and intellectual infection *did* occur and was probably too high a price to pay for modernization; moreover, as several characters like Obodovsky suggest in *August 1914*, that same transformation was underway *without* the stifling repression and enforced conformity of which Heilbroner speaks.

During the dinner table conversation, Obodovsky, experienced in such situations, keeps his temper as Sonya and Naum continue to bait him, but Arkhangorodsky is annoyed and embarrassed by the young people's gall, and so, sounding like the father he is, says things like this: "There are thousands of you, none of you has done any work for a long time, it's not done to ask where your money comes from. . . ." (667) and this: "it's easier to shout and it's more fun to make a revolution than to build Russia up. That's too much like hard work" (669) and this: "Don't imagine that a republic automatically means bread and circuses for all. What would happen? A hundred ambitious lawyers would assemble—and who talks more hot air than lawyers do?—and shout each other down" (669). Arkhangorodsky is being only a trifle more earthy and explicit than a number of other thoughtful people in *August 1914* who indict the revolutionaries.

The revolutionaries would rather talk and theorize than work, and this at a time when there *is* constructive work to do. They want the fun and glamor of being revolutionaries, but they also want to be excused from ordinary people's demands upon their attention and sympathy. "Individual instances of so-called compassion," says Ensign Lenartovich, "only obscure the issue and delay a general solution of the problem" (163). They are as bad as the incompetent generals safely behind the front lines. As Arkhangorodsky says:

> "On one side—the Black hundreds; on the other—the Red hundreds! And in the middle—" he formed his hands into the shape of a ship's keel— "a dozen people who want to pass through to get on with a job of work! Impossible!" He opened his hands and clapped them together. "They are crushed—flattened!" (672)

There are considerably more than a dozen people who see what needs to be done, and a large portion of *August 1914* demonstrates how much even a single man (Colonel Vorotýntsev) can do. But when so many members of the intelligentsia, believing that politics and ideological purity come before hard work, fail to support the creators (and indeed are contemptuous of unromantic, bourgeois mill builders like Arkhangorodsky and dedicated officers like Vorotýntsev), then the creators *will* fail. They can nearly do it all alone—but not quite.

Chapter 58 pinpoints even further the prevailing attitudes of the confident young. Olda Orestovna Andozerskaya, a professor specializing in the middle ages, is asked by one of her students, "Surely for practical purposes all we need today is an analysis of the contemporary social environment and material conditions?" Andozerskaya sees the alluring simplicity of that formula and replies:

> "That would be so if the life of the individual really

190

were determined by his material environment. It would be much easier then: the environment is always at fault, so all you have to do is change it. But apart from the environment there is also a spiritual tradition, hundreds of spiritual traditions! There is, too, the spiritual life of the *individual*, and therefore each individual has, perhaps in spite of his environment, a *personal* responsibility —for what he does and for what other people around him do" (631).

Few of the students are interested. But Veronika, Ensign Lenartovich's beautiful sister, asks, "For other people too?" as if it is a new and stimulating idea. She is described as a "fresco coming alive," and one suspects that like so many other characters who appear only briefly in *August 1914* Solzhenitsyn has plans for her in future volumes. Her fellow students, however, regard individuality and personal responsibility as quaint and idealistic concepts. But the defeat of Olda Orestovna's (and Solzhenitsyn's) viewpoint in favor of the Marxist theory that, as another eager-to-be-realistic student puts it, "We are molecules of the environment and that's that" (631), will damage Russia as much as the war will. Or so *August 1914* predicts. The younger generation of intellectuals is preparing itself, sometimes unwittingly, to submit to those who will want to manipulate those molecules.

Earlier, Pavel Ivanovich Varsonofiev, one of those older and wiser men who have a habit of appearing at crucial moments in Solzhenitsyn's work, is discussing life with Kotya and Sanya. Like Sologdin in *The First Circle* and Shulubin in *Cancer Ward*, Varsonofiev speaks partly with calm authority (as if Solzhenitsyn is fully behind him) and partly like a pompous lecturing professor (as if Solzhenitsyn wants to show again how easily thinkers become dogmatists). But we know Solzhenitsyn agrees when Varsonofiev, himself sounding like Olda Orestovna, says that the often-used word "develop" has not only a social application but

191

"a better and more important application—we should develop our *soul*. There is nothing more precious than the development of a man's own soul; it is more important than the well-being of countless future generations" (473).

By this time any experienced reader of Solzhenitsyn needs no explanation of "soul." But Kotya and Sanya are worried: If men do set about developing their souls, what happens to "the social order," with which every young intellectual in *August 1914* is concerned? Varsonofiev replies:

"Obviously one kind is less evil than all the others. Perhaps there may even be a perfect one. Only remember, my friends, that the best social order is not susceptible to being arbitrarily constructed, or even to being scientifically constructed—everything is allegedly scientific nowadays. Do not be so arrogant as to imagine that you can invent an ideal social order, because with that invention you may destroy your beloved 'people' " (474).

Solzhenitsyn's other novels show us that such a destruction did occur.

Varsonofiev goes on to explain his theory of history—it is "irrational," it has its own "perhaps incomprehensible, organic structure" (474)—and while his explanation becomes increasingly vague, it is not because he is confused. He just knows that not everything, least of all "history," can be explained by easily understood laws and formulas. He is yet another example in Solzhenitsyn's work of a man who recognizes genuine mystery when he sees it, knows that people have lived on this earth before now, and warns against human arrogance when he can.

It is worth recalling that the practical-minded good men in *August 1914* like Obodovsky and Arkhangorodsky are indeed interested in making plans which sound dangerously close to what Varsonofiev is against. Obodovsky likes to imagine how much could be accomplished "in ten years, and how much in twenty, by the application of a single, integrated plan in which each step was related to future developments" (656); he also believes that "the Union of Engineers could easily become one of the leading forces in Russia" (658). The pressing need to modernize the country, which practically everyone in the novel recognizes (except those who control the military), gives words like "science" and "engineer" and terms like "integrated plan" almost magical connotations. After the revolution, those who enthusiastically support science and proper planning (unless they themselves become too powerful, or unless a scapegoat for a state failure is needed) will be far more influential than those who bleat about the "soul" or "individual responsibility."

But in *August 1914* Solzhenitsyn does not make the Varsonofievs and Olda Orestovnas into adversaries of the engineers any more than he pits the professional soldiers like Colonel Vorotýntsev against theoretical pacifists like Sanya. The reader senses that all these people could sit down together and agree that competence, personal responsibility, foresight, and morality are necessary for Russia's well-being. Their common foe is extreme ideology. Extreme ideology leads to polarization; it will set people to arguing when they should be working; and ultimately it will foster a state which will have to exclude (as socially undesirable, as "class enemies") large numbers of potentially productive people. In *August 1914* there is still room at the same table for the star-gazing Varsonofiev, the practical mill builder and the competent military man. All are clear-sighted enough to see that each has something to offer, and none are imprisoned by ideology. It may be that eventually Obodovsky and Arkhangorodsky *will* make a religion of applied science and become like some of those easily manipulated technocrats in *The First Circle* who are in love with their work for its own sake, but for now they want only to use their skills on projects which will undeniably benefit their country. One of the more general messages of *August 1914* is

193

that Russia needs what all countries need: a few more decent, competent, hard-working people in the right places. Among such people the recognition of the need to modernize in some areas of life, including the need to have a modern, efficient military, is not concomitant with denying moral or spiritual values. Throughout the novel, when the subject is war and food production, Solzhenitsyn praises efficiency, organization, and technology, but at the same time he supports the old-fashioned moral imperatives.[9] That there may be such a thing as a technological imperative which can knock askew old-fashioned morality is not a proposition he entertains.

In *August 1914* morality and efficiency are closely related. Once Russia is actually at war, it is apparent to everyone except the most perverse revolutionaries that, as Varsonofiev says, "For some reason it is important that Russia's backbone not be broken" (476). The novel is not intended as a lament over Russia's failure to win a decisive victory at Tannenberg, nor does Solzhenitsyn suggest that Russia necessarily enters the war with truth and justice on her side. But once the fighting begins, soldiers on every level *are* obligated to do the best they can. It is one thing to be defeated, but quite another to be *slaughtered* in defeat as a result of incompetence among those in charge. Even with the best strategic and tactical leadership, Russia probably would have been defeated— but not as badly. At that moment in history, industrialized Germany had a definite technological advantage (armored vehicles, longer-range artillery, more airplanes, etc.) whereas Russia's only advantage, according to *August 1914*, was the courage and toughness (and sheer numbers and rifle-shooting ability) of her common soldiers.[10]

But despite his occasional generalizations about the unpreparedness of the country for war, Solzhenitsyn's main emphasis, as usual, is to indict individual *men*— men whom he can *name*—for not fulfilling their responsibilities, for not doing what was in their power to do.

194

August 1914 carefully describes large numbers of *specific* correctable failures. There was no agreed-upon plan of battle; the troops were often marched about aimlessly to the point of exhaustion and separated from their supplies; the officers in the field were without proper maps and without reliable means of communicating with their superiors; when telephonic communications *were* available, the Russians sent uncoded, easily intercepted messages; there was a consistent misuse, and sometimes even a withholding, of artillery and cavalry at decisive moments; several of the generals were outright liars when reporting their positions or the condition of their troops. And the list goes on. Although some critics believe that General Samsonov himself is invested with a kind of tragic grandeur, most of *August 1914* is a record of small, careless mistakes which add up to an ignominious defeat, a rout. The reader is left brimming with exasperation, not purged by any grand and stately emotions. In the final chapter, in reply to his friend Svechin who is urging him to examine the whole picture before reporting to the general staff, Colonel Vorotýntsev says:

"I agree that a defeat in one sector can be counterbalanced by success somewhere else. But this isn't a military problem any longer, don't you see? It's a *moral* issue. To drive one's people unprepared to slaughter is something far beyond the considerations of mere strategy. . . . And none of *them* even go to the front line to see for themselves!" (692–93)

In *August 1914* Solzhenitsyn's envy of German efficiency, technology, and modernization is understandable, and right. In war there is no substitute for them. In his earlier works, written about time-periods when the ideals of efficiency, technology, and modernization have won the day and all sorts of crimes are now being committed in the name of these ideals, Solzhenitsyn's skepticism of them is also understandable and right.

Svechin gives Vorotýntsev the kind of sensible advice of which almost anyone is capable:

> "Even so, you won't do any good," Svechin insisted firmly, hissing the words through clenched teeth. "Nothing would be changed and you'd simply get a bloody nose. Russia is doomed to be governed by fools; she knows no other way. I know what I'm talking about. The only thing to do is keep your head down and get on with the job" (693).

As all Solzhenitsyn's heroes do, Vorotýntsev must act on his knowledge of what is morally correct, and so he will not keep his head down (as his subsequent verbal attack on the general staff shows). It is easy enough to intone about Russia, or any country, that, yes, she will be governed by fools—such generalizations are common in Solzhenitsyn's work, frequently uttered in his own naked prophetic voice. But at the same time he always champions those like Vorotýntsev who do not accept those predictions as inevitable.

That so many men like these were killed, broken, or demoralized by the war was a terrible loss to Russia and one of the reasons that after the war new fools continued to govern. As Solzhenitsyn says at the beginning of Chapter 40, one of his essays-within-a-novel:

> Who can undertake to name the decisive battle in a war that lasted four years and strained the nation's morale to breaking point? Of the countless battles, more ended in ignominy than in renown, devouring our strength and our faith in ourselves, uselessly and irretrievably snatching from us our bravest and strongest men and leaving the second-raters (440).

Much of the novel shows us these brave and strong men from every level of society doing their duty as best they can, and we know that *August 1914* is partly intended as a memorial to them just as the prison novels and parts of

The Gulag Archipelago memorialize other brave and strong men who might have been forgotten. Solzhenitsyn focuses particularly on that fraternity of career officers at the rank of major, lieutenant colonel, or colonel (plus a handful of generals with obscure commands) who are too selfless and dedicated to have made it to the top. It is this group which tries to salvage what it can from the wreckage. At the town of Neidenburg, Colonel Vorotýntsev has assembled a few of them:

> In a few sentences Vorotýntsev explained to these two lieutenant colonels and to half the surviving company commanders the situation of the town, the situation of the army, the fact that their regimental commander had retreated back to Russia along with the remaining companies of their regiment, and the job that he wanted the rest of them to do. As he spoke, he looked into their faces and saw, as though in his own features, that fundamentally they all bore the indelible impress of a similar background: army tradition; long spells of garrison service in a world isolated from the rest of society; a sense of alienation, of being despised by that society and ridiculed by liberal writers; the official ban on discussing politics and political literature, resulting in a blunting or stultifying of the intellect; a permanent shortage of money; and yet, despite it all, the knowledge that they represented, in purified and concentrated form, the vitality and courage of the whole nation (412).

They are capable of effective *ad hoc* action. Had men like them been in command of the entire operation, the outcome at Tannenberg would have been less disastrous; had more of them survived, Russia's future would have been brighter. Maybe.

But it would be an oversimplification to say that Solzhenitsyn is regretting the loss of a military elite which could have taken charge of the war and later of the entire country any more than he is unreservedly regretting the loss

197

of an elite group of industrial and agricultural managers represented in the novel by Obodovsky and Zakhar Tomchak. The concept of an elite is misleading. In addition to their special talents, these officers have a moral authority based on their knowledge and their love of the men under their command. Although sometimes amused and sometimes surprised by them, they do not regard themselves as intrinsically superior to their men (Ensign Lenartovich, the revolutionary, *does*). In *August 1914* military competence is synonymous with a form of love, a high sense of responsibility for the lives of others. Without exception the best officers take their men seriously, try to talk to as many as they can, try to insure that they have proper meals, enough rest, and suitable equipment, try to gain a feel for their morale and spirit. They stay close to the trenches and to the front line; the farther back they are from the actual fighting, the more likely they are to regard troops as chessmen and therefore to make serious miscalculations about the army's strengths and weaknesses.

At Neidenburg, when it is necessary for the already exhausted Estland regiment to plug a gap in the lines so that others can retreat, Vorotýntsev knows that to make a fancy speech to the men would only insult their intelligence. "As he gazed at the rows of grim, tired, sullen faces, he put himself in their place, draped in their sweaty greatcoat rolls, in sweaty shirts and leather straps that cut into their shoulders, in their hot boots with the reek of unwashed feet" (414). He puts himself in their place and gives a short, honest explanation of the situation and the men in turn "saw and felt his utter sincerity" (415). In this case perhaps the men's willingness to sacrifice themselves is too good to be true ("Isn't it selfish," asks Vorotýntsev, "to save ourselves at the expense of others?"), but the scene is nevertheless the most dramatic of many examples in *August 1914* of a good officer and good men mutually respecting one another.

We are repeatedly made aware that apart from the superiority of the German army the Russians lost Tannenberg because their generals, like so many of the bureaucrats in *The First Circle* and *Cancer Ward*, are out of touch with the actual lives of those they are supposed to be managing. Certainly the generals need not (indeed should not) be literally in the trenches, but they should know the basic needs of their men. In describing the German General von François's preparations for an attack, Solzhenitsyn, in a bitter backhanded slap at the Russian failure in this regard, notes that von François's "detachments were to be closely followed by mobile field kitchens, to keep them fed. (A good commander always remembered his soldiers' rations)" (427). Von François then goes forward "to observe and direct the departing Brigade." Although von François makes mistakes (at one point he is so far forward that, in a triumph of fiction over fact, he and Colonel Vorotýntsev meet face to face) and is overly conscious of his place in history (he keeps written records of every move he makes, which Solzhenitsyn obviously consulted), he does not leave the details to others:

> Unusually agile and energetic for his age, he was a man who fought his battles with élan and flair; he would climb up into belfries for observation, supervise the unloading of shells under fire (although they would probably have been unloaded well enough without his help), and visit every part of the battlefield by car to insure that his orders were being carried out, sometimes going for a whole day sustained by nothing but a cup of cocoa (this was for the benefit of his memoirs; he did not record the number of steaks he ate), often sleeping no more than two or three hours a night (249).

The Russian General Artamonov also drives around in a car, but that is because "he honestly could not think of anything better to do" (257). At one point when Artamonov is about to take another drive, Solzhenitsyn questions and speculates:

199

What arrangements had he made for headquarters to function in his absence? Who was in charge of intelligence? What communications were there between the artillery and the infantry? How many rounds per gun had been brought forward, and were there enough ammunition boxes and wagons to keep the gunners supplied during the battle? He probably didn't know, and was not even aware that he ought to (260).

It is neglect of detail on this scale which is inexcusable.

The two men officially responsible for the Tannenberg debacle are Grand Duke Nikolai Nikolaevich and General Samsonov, both of whom *do* know the importance of detail, of first-hand information, of the condition of the army on the battlefield rather than on the headquarters map. Nikolai Nikolaevich is aware that his staff is no good (better men were available but he acceded to the will of the Tsar) and likely to mislead him and that is why he sends Colonel Vorotýntsev—"the man he needed more than anyone else" (680)—to the front to be his eyes and ears. That does some good, but not much. The Grand Duke is too far away.

Closer to the scene, General Samsonov knows perfectly well what he should do:

> He wanted to get the feel of the ground, to walk around the little town and inspect it on foot. He wanted to put his new location on the map and reexamine his dispositions; to see how near his formations were to him, by what routes they could be reached, which of them were linked to him by telegraph, and where the lines ran (191).

Early in the novel we learn that Samsonov felt the "mileage on the soles of his men's boots as if they were his own . . ." (96). Later when he discovers that some of his troops have not eaten any hardtack for three days, he nearly collapses:

200

It would have been a relief to have fallen to his knees and cried out: "I am the culprit—I sent you to your destruction!" A weight would have fallen from his heart if he could have taken all the guilt on himself and risen to his feet no longer the army commander.

Instead, he calmly gave the order: "Feed them all at once. And send them to the rear for a rest period."

But his burden grew no less, and Samsonov walked back into town, stumbling like a man under a curse (339).

That he has a conscience is scant consolation. But he is one Russian general who *does* love his troops, and he bitterly regrets his failure to act decisively on that love.

Not only are Samsonov's superiors at the Northwestern Army Group incompetent but, like the Grand Duke, he is surrounded by an incompetent staff not of his own choosing, facts which Solzhenitsyn meticulously documents. Indeed, when he meets the truly able Colonel Vorotýntsev, Samsonov is awakened and refreshed, and for a time it seems that with the support of even one or two intelligent subordinates he might be able to do the job. But he does not—even though he loves his men. And Solzhenitsyn, while providing several good reasons for Samsonov's poor performance, does not excuse him. The general's heart is in the right place, but his mind and will are elsewhere—and Solzhenitsyn's portrait of him is, up to a point, interesting because he makes Samsonov's failings both commonplace and rather complicated, almost as if he is not a general at all. By the time Samsonov is ready to commit suicide, after he has begun to have visions and hear voices, Solzhenitsyn seems not to know what to do with the general and so *does* reduce him to an easily explained figure in a trance:

He was no longer surrounded by an earthly foe, no longer threatened; he had risen above all such perils. The cloud which darkened the army commander's brow was not, after all, one of guilt but one of ineffable greatness: perhaps outwardly he had done things which were wrong by the petty canons of strategy and tactics, but from his point of view, what he had done had been profoundly right (498).

Before this point Samsonov is portrayed as a man who is well aware that he is engaged in the most important enterprise of his life, and yet he continually allows himself to be distracted by the smallest things. Total concentration and absolute self-discipline are necessary in this life-and-death situation, and he knows it. But he cannot achieve "the mental clarity he longed for" (185), and in this respect he has our sympathy. It is a very common problem. Solzhenitsyn does give him at least this excuse: He was "under orders to execute in haste a plan that was not only not of his own devising but which he had not even had time to study." In *August 1914* the word "time" has almost as much weight as the word "competent":

> Above all, he needed to be alone for a while, to order his thoughts, to weigh the plan and study the maps; but for none of this was he granted the time. The new commander needed to get to know his staff and find out which of them would make good advisers and assistants; but there had been no time to spare for this either (88–89).

Nevertheless, in any war there is seldom enough time, and the best generals work effectively even under this handicap. Samsonov's basic failing is his own:

> He did not precisely know why his thoughts were still unclear: all the necessary orders had been issued and were being carried out, yet there was a blur, a kind of undissipated fog of overlapping, unfocused globs that danced in front of his inward eye as though he had double vision. Samsonov was continually conscious of this and it worried him greatly (185).

Phrases like "a kind of undissipated fog" and "unfocused globs" are quite precise enough to describe a phenomenon that ultimately cannot be easily explained. In a situation where an extraordinary man is needed there is only an ordinary man who is unable to cope with distraction. In Chapter 17, as he is being accompanied by the English General Knox (whom Solzhenitsyn sees as a source of further distraction to Samsonov and therefore partly to blame for the Tannenberg defeat), Samsonov

> took the map board from his knees and leaned it against the door of the car. His strength drained by all these explanations and by the growing heat, he no longer felt a desire to reflect in private or to study the terrain; he only wanted to be able to doze in his comfortable seat (188).

It is a shocking failure of will. The best of the Russian generals, Martos, a front-line general, a man with imagination, self-discipline, and a sense of detail, finds himself in a similar situation when facing von Scholtz's troops near Waplitz:

> He put himself in von Scholtz's place, mentally running over the situation of the past day. Yes, von Scholtz's corps would now be facing in a suitable direction and the time was right.
> Although the general's body now felt ready to drop asleep, somewhere within him a little warning light flashed. He went indoors, woke up his lazy and reluctant staff officers, and called up the orderlies by telephone (380).

No matter how elaborate the historical and political reasons Solzhenitsyn gives for the twists and turns of the battle, he is most painfully credible when he shows how much the outcome was determined by the character of individual men.

The moment we are introduced to General Samsonov at his headquarters in Ostrolenka, we realize that he needs help. Then Vorotýntsev appears and gives a temporary sense of security to Samsonov, and to us. In any novel where everyone is threatened with annihilation, it is a distinct pleasure for the reader to have one person on whom he can depend, who he knows will withstand the ever increasing pressure. Vorotýntsev is a hero—which, as we have seen before in Solzhenitsyn's work, is not a vague literary concept but the sum of a particular man's acts under particular circumstances. Solzhenitsyn gives Vorotýntsev enough faults and personal problems to make him interesting, carefully describes his practical knowledge to show us why he is so proficient at his job, and never allows us to forget the moral dimension of Vorotýntsev's character. At the onset Colonel Vorotýntsev is *prepared* to be a hero, and as the novel unfolds he becomes even more of one. (He is also a device which ties together disparate elements in the novel.) It is true that unlike the majority of officers in any army at any time he is given the luxury of being attached to no specific unit except the distant General Staff and can therefore choose his own arena for action, but this does not invalidate his portrait, though it occasionally places it in jeopardy.

Vorotýntsev's actions fall into a pattern: He surveys the situation, tries to repair it, moves on, witnesses more chaos and confusion until he finds another situation to repair, does his best, moves on again, and so forth. From time to time, when he or some other man like him starts to work, we recover our feelings of security and hope, as if at a way station, but then we are promptly plunged again into the frustrating position of watching mistake after mistake pile up. Eventually, a reservoir of indignation gradually forms in both Vorotýntsev and the reader. At the end when Vorotýntsev makes his report to the General Staff, he becomes a prosecutor and a judge, which is very satisfying but still does not release all our indignation. Although *August 1914* is full of excitement, adventure, and many examples of heroism, it also leaves us aware of individual moral failures and incompetencies and, as so often in Solzhenitsyn, knowing exactly where to place the blame.[11]

Despite the pains Solzhenitsyn takes to make Vorotýntsev a credible hero and moral spokesman, he is also a projection of the author's own longing for a man who can do everything. Solzhenitsyn surely puts some of his own aspirations into Vorotýntsev's portrait:

> Ever since his youth, Vorotýntsev had been obsessed by one profound desire: to be a good influence on the history of his country, either by pushing it or by pulling it—by the roots of the hair if necessary!—in the right direction. But in Russia that kind of power and influence were not granted to anyone who was not fortunate enough to be close to the throne; at whatever point Vorotýntsev attempted to exert pressure and however much he exhausted himself trying, the effort was always in vain (267).

One could argue that the end of *August 1914* shows Vorotýntsev's effort indeed to be in vain, but very few readers would say the same about Solzhenitsyn's own effort to be a good influence on the history of his country.

A FINAL COMMENT

At this point it may seem appropriate to devise a "Solzhenitsyn" who stands above and beyond individual characters and scenes, who takes a definite, definable position as he gazes upon mankind. We know by now that he challenges the fondest assumptions of many educated people: Morality is relative, good and evil are meaningless terms, religion is an opiate, material well-being is the aim of life, science will save us, social science will explain us, true wisdom manifests itself in silent toleration of practically anything. But if Solzhenitsyn hesitates to accept these assumptions, what *does* he assume? How can we "place" him? Is he a Christian, a moralist, an individualist, a Russian patriot, an anti-Sovietist? One could extend this list and say that Solzhenitsyn is all these things and more, such a multi-voiced writer that he resists categorical description—but that is not true, either. I will, however, say this: Like all good novelists when they are

206

being novelists and not something else, Solzhenitsyn is interested in the details of how people live their lives, and when he is at his best his characters do defy categorization. They become unique, particularized individuals—and it would be misleading to claim that his conception of them is based on a Christian, or conservative, or anti-Marxist, or other "view" of mankind. Best to let the characters shift for themselves in our memory without conceptual support.

When Solzhenitsyn is not being a novelist but rather an unashamed revealer of himself, as in the following passage from *Gulag Two*, parts of which I have used before, we are at liberty, I suppose, to call him anything we like:

> It was granted me to carry away from my prison years on my bent back, which nearly broke beneath its load, this essential experience: *how* a human being becomes evil and *how* good. In the intoxication of youthful successes I had felt myself to be infallible, and I was therefore cruel. In the surfeit of power I was a murderer, and an oppressor. In my most evil moments I was convinced that I was doing good, and I was well supplied with systematic arguments. And it was only when I lay there on rotting prison straw that I sensed within myself the first stirrings of good. Gradually it was disclosed to me that the line separating good and evil passes not through states, nor between classes, nor between political parties either—but right through every human heart—and through all human hearts. The line shifts. Inside us, it oscillates with the years. And even within hearts overwhelmed by evil, one small bridgehead of good is retained. And even in the best of all hearts, there remains . . . an unuprooted small corner of evil.
>
> Since then I have come to understand the truth of all the religions of the world: They struggle with the *evil inside a human being* (inside every human being). It is impossible to expel evil from the world in its entirety, but it is possible to constrict it within each person.
>
> And since that time I have come to understand the

falsehood of all the revolutions in history: They destroy only *those carriers* of evil contemporary with them (and also fail, out of haste, to discriminate the carriers of good as well). And they then take to themselves as their heritage the actual evil itself, magnified still more (615–16).

I would add only that in Solzhenitsyn's fiction (as well as in many case histories in *Gulag I* and *II*) the concept of "evil" is given flesh and blood, and Solzhenitsyn's use of the term is earned. It is not a mark of intellectual laziness.

Even without the evidence of *The Gulag Archipelago*, among the most extensive and important catalogues of human error ever written, we sense in Solzhenitsyn's pages a pressing urgency to tell the unvarnished truth rather than to shape his facts to fit an ideology, even a Christian ideology, if such a thing may be said to exist. Before his time runs out he wants to tell the truth about *everything*, about the entire life of his country in the twentieth century. He knows as well as we do that the task is too great for any one man, but if he does not try, who will? No American writer has ever had such a flaming sense of mission; none has ever had to. Despite our frequent outbreaks of paranoia and self-laceration, in this country we have never come close to the condition described below, which is as good a motive for becoming a novelist as I have ever seen:

> Hiding things from each other, and not trusting each other, we ourselves helped implement that *absolute secrecy*, absolute misinformation, among us which was *the cause of causes* of everything that took place—including both the millions of arrests and the mass approval of them also. Informing one another of nothing, neither shouting nor groaning, and learning nothing from one another, we were completely in the hands of the newspapers and the official orators. Every day they pushed in our faces some new piece of incitement, like

a photograph of a railroad wreck (sabotage) somewhere three thousand miles away. And what we really needed to learn about, which was what had happened on our apartment landing that day, we had no way of finding out.

How could you become a citizen, knowing nothing about life around you? Only when you yourself were caught in the trap would you find out—too late (*Gulag II*, 636).

Solzhenitsyn's fiction shows us what happened on the apartment landing that day and why it happened. His characters are the specific results of his desire to inform, to tell the truth.

Twentieth-century Russia has been imprisoned by ideology, in particular an ideology which values ends rather than means:

And ever more firmly it became established among a once pious and openhearted people: The result is what counts.

And then—from all kinds of socialists, and most of all from the most modern, infallible, and intolerant Teaching, which consists of this one thing only: The result is what counts! It is important to forge a fighting Party! And to seize power! And to hold on to power! And to remove all enemies! And to conquer in pig iron and steel! And to launch rockets!

And though for this industry and for these rockets it was necessary to sacrifice the way of life, and the integrity of the family, and the spiritual health of the people, and the very soul of our fields and forests and rivers—to hell with them! The result is what counts!!!

But that is a lie! Here we have been breaking our backs for years at All-Union hard labor. Here in slow annual spirals we have been climbing up to an understanding of life—and from this height it can all be seen so clearly: It is not the result that counts! It is not the result—but *the spirit!* Not *what*—but *how*. Not what has been attained—but at what price (*Gulag II*, 609).

209

As we have seen, words like "spirit," "love," and "soul" are the key affirmative words in Solzhenitsyn's fiction. They are old, worn, hard to define, and easily misused, but Solzhenitsyn gives them new life and makes us see that such terms *do* house real wisdom—you either believe that and admire him or you don't believe it and patronize him.

Solzhenitsyn approvingly quotes the "drastic, sweeping declaration" of M. A. Voichenko:

> "In camp, existence did not determine consciousness, but just the opposite: consciousness and steadfast faith in the human essence decided whether you became an animal or remained a human being" (*Gulag II*, 626).

It comes down to this: The Marxist-Leninist-Stalinist ideological tradition, with all its associated institutions, taints everything it touches and is fundamentally mistaken about human nature. The most admirable characters in Solzhenitsyn's fiction—Ivan Denisovich, Oleg Kostoglotov, Gleb Nerzhin, Colonel Vorotýntsev—resist this tradition and its institutions. They choose truth above ideology and fight for freedom when they can.

FOOTNOTES TO PREFACE

[1] In the summer of 1976 Solzhenitsyn's name was repeatedly invoked at the Republican National Convention, but, as Max Lerner wrote in his syndicated column (25 August 1976), probably not "half the delegates on the floor knew more about Solzhenitsyn than his name. . . ."

[2] "Looking for Kellerman; or Fiction and the Facts of Life," in *The Theory of the Novel*, ed. John Helperin (New York, 1974), pp. 274–275.

[3] See Ehre's "On *August 1914*," Carpovich's "Lexical Peculiarities of Solzhenitsyn's Language," and Struve's "The Debate Over *August 1914*," all in *Aleksandr Solzhenitsyn: Critical Essays and Documentary Materials*, ed. John B. Dunlop, Richard Haugh, and Alexis Klimoff (Belmont, Mass., 1973), pp. 371, 188, 405, respectively. This book will hereafter be cited as *Dunlop*.

[4] *Dunlop*, p. 557.

FOOTNOTES TO CHAPTER ONE

One Day in the Life of
Ivan Denisovich

[1] *One Day in the Life of Ivan Denisovich*, Max Hayward and Ronald Hingley, trans. (New York: Bantam, 1963), p. 14. Subsequent references to this edition will be included in the text.

[2] "The Heroism of Survival," in *Dunlop*, pp. 52–53.

[3] Although Hemingway is occasionally mentioned in his work, I do not intend to suggest that Solzhenitsyn necessarily admires him. In *Cancer Ward*, for example, he has Vera Gangart reflect that "Hemingway's supermen were creatures who had not yet raised themselves to human level. Hemingway was a shallow swimmer" (p. 342).

[4] "On Solzhenitsyn," in *Dunlop*, p. 42.

[5] *The Gulag Archipelago Two*, Thomas P. Whitney, trans.

(New York: Harper & Row, 1975), p. 258. Subsequent references to this edition will be included in the text.

[6] As a matter of history, there were of course ways the prison authorities could improve efficiency, at least temporarily. One was the institution of the "shock brigade" full of "shock workers," who were supposed to be motivated by pure love of work and country (note the picture of their smiling faces in *Gulag II*). What really made them work was the promise of more food. See *Gulag II*, pp. 103–120.

[7] In *The First Circle*, there is this description of Gleb Nerzhin and a use of the term "economy": "His skin looked faded because of the lack of fresh air. But it was most of all his economy of movement that made him seem old—that wise economy with which nature husbands a prisoner's strength against the drain of a concentration-camp regime. True, in the relative freedom of the sharashka, where the diet included meat and energy wasn't burned up in physical labor, there was no real need for economy of movement . . ." (22)

[8] See "On Solzhenitsyn," in *Dunlop*, pp. 28–44.

[9] *TLS* (11 April 1975), 886.

FOOTNOTES TO CHAPTER TWO

The First Circle

[1] *Solzhenitsyn*, William David Graf, trans. (Cambridge, Mass., 1971), pp. 42–43. Lukács's book is worth reading for its interesting distinction between the novella and the novel. Ultimately he criticizes Solzhenitsyn for continuing to write from the "plebeian" rather than the socialist perspective. Lukács himself often sounds like the character Lev Rubin in *The First Circle*. See also Irving Howe's discussion of Lukács's career: *Dissent* (Dec. 1971), 643–647.

[2] *Solzhenitsyn*, trans. Eric Mosbacher (London, 1973), pp. 110 and 112.

[3] From an interview in Georges Nivat and Michael Ancouturier, eds., *Soljénitsyne* (Paris, 1971), p. 118.

[4] *The Nobel Lecture on Literature*, Thomas P. Whitney, trans. (New York: Harper & Row, 1972), p. 36. Subsequent references to this edition will be included in the text.

[5] *The First Circle*, Thomas P. Whitney, trans. (New York: Bantam, 1969), p. 9. Subsequent references to this edition will be included in the text.

[6] "The Role of the Lie in *The First Circle*," in *Dunlop*, p. 265.

[7] *Solzhenitsyn*, p. 107.

[8] *Art and Reality* (New York, 1958), p. 23.

[9] *Ibid.*

[10] Gleb Zekulin, however, makes a plausible case for Solzhenitsyn's works being read in a quite different sequence than I use in this book. According to Zekulin, the most illuminating "order of progression" is: *The Love-Girl and the Innocent, The First Circle, Ivan Denisovich, Cancer Ward, A Candle in the Wind.* See "The Plays of Aleksandr Solzhenitsyn," in *Dunlop*, pp. 303–16.

[11] *Art and Reality*, p. 165.

[12] See the fourth unnumbered page of the "Preface" to *The Screwtape Letters/Screwtape Proposes a Toast* (New York, 1961).

[13] *Aleksandr Solzhenitsyn: A Biography*, Kaarina Eneberg, trans. (New York, 1972), p. 30.

[14] "The Writer as Witness: The Achievement of Aleksandr Solzhenitsyn," in *Dunlop*, pp. 24–25.

[15] Not everyone, of course, believes that Marx misapprehended human nature. For a lucid defense of his humanism, see Erich Fromm, *Marx's Concept of Man* (New York, 1961).

[16] Joan Didion, "On Morality," in *Slouching Towards Bethlehem* (New York, 1968), p. 162.

[17] *Time* (April 5, 1976), 26.

[18] "The Odyssey of a Skeptic: Gleb Nerzhin," in *Dunlop*, p. 247.

[19] See Emerson's "The American Scholar" or "Self-Reliance." Not only in Sologdin's portrait but throughout Solzhenitsyn there are interesting similarities between his thought and the American Transcendentalists' writings.

[20] According to Lukács, the "rich and variegated light thrown on the inner life of an epoch (the era of Stalin's last years, following the break with Tito) produces no real changes, either subjectively in the characters or objectively in society" (*Solzhenitsyn*, p. 65).

215

FOOTNOTES TO CHAPTER THREE

Cancer Ward

[1] For a considerably different view of the forces influencing modern economic history than that offered by Marx, see Weber's classic study, *The Protestant Ethic and The Spirit of Capitalism* (1904–5).

[2] *Cancer Ward*, Nicholas Bethell and David Burg, trans. (New York: Bantam, 1969), p. 23. Subsequent references to this edition will be included in the text.

[3] Although Burg and Feifer cast it in the past tense, there is no reason to regard their point as past history. See their *Solzhenitsyn*, p. 240.

[4] Quoted in Burg and Feifer, *Solzhenitsyn*, p. 240.

[5] *Candle in the Wind*, Keith Armes, trans. (New York: Bantam Books, 1974), p. 110. Subsequent references to this edition will be included in the text.

216

[6] See Burg and Feifer, *Solzhenitsyn*, p. 122.

[7] *"Cancer Ward*: of Fate and Guilt," in *Dunlop*, p. 284.

[8] *Ibid.*, p. 286.

[9] *Ibid.*, p. 289.

[10] *Ibid.*, pp. 282–283.

[11] "The Writer as Witness: The Achievement of Aleksander Solzhenitsyn," in *Dunlop*, p. 22.

FOOTNOTES TO CHAPTER FOUR

August 1914

[1] See Mary McCarthy, "The Tolstoy Connection," in *Dunlop*, p. 332, and Victor Erlich, "Solzhenitsyn's Quest," in *Dunlop*, p. 352. Erlich also asserts that the novel "lacks the firmness of outline, the sureness of touch, in a word, the authority of *One Day in the Life of Ivan Denisovich* or *The First Circle*. The prose is not infrequently contrived and unwieldy." On the contrary, the prose of *August 1914* is fluid and flexible, as if Solzhenitsyn is skiing downhill all the way.

[2] Solzhenitsyn's father fought in this same region. Solzhenitsyn himself served in the artillery here in World War Two. When he was a student in the late 1930s he did an extensive research project on the 1914 Russian campaign in East Prussia. For the definitive account of Solzhenitsyn's amazingly accurate use of sources, see Dorothy Atkinson's "*August 1914*: Historical Novel or Novel History," in *Dunlop*, pp. 408–429.

[3] *August 1914*, Michael Glenny, trans. (New York: Bantam,

1974), p. 1. Subsequent references to this edition will be included in the text.

[4] See Knox's *With the Russian Army, 1914–1917* (London, 1921), I, xxxiv.

[5] For example:

> But from the first battle on, a Russian general's badges of rank come to be seen as symbols of incompetence; and the further up the hierarchy, the more bungling the generals seem, until there is scarcely one from whom an anthor can derive any comfort. (In which case there might appear to be some consolation in Tolstoy's conviction that it is not generals who lead armies, not captains who command ships or companies of infantry, not presidents or leaders who run states or political parties —were it not that all too often the twentieth century has proved to us that it *is* such men who do these things.) (441)

[6] "*August 1914*: Solzhenitsyn and Tolstoy," in *Dunlop*, p. 375.

[7] In his article "Behind the Front Lines: On Some Neglected Chapters in *August 1914*," Gleb Struve quotes from a letter to him from Nikolai Vladislavovich Vol'skii (N. Valentinov, author of *Encounters with Lenin* [1968]):

> Yes, Gleb Petrovich, the period 1908–1914, extremely interesting in the history of Russia, has so far failed, alas, to find an historian. Many people, let alone the Bolsheviks, see it as standing under the sign of "dark reaction" and of court-martials. This is a complete distortion of reality. This period saw a remarkable growth of industry (had there been no interruption, its level would be equal to that of Soviet industry today!); housing in the cities was growing on an enormous scale; land was passing, in huge chunks, into the hands of thrifty peasants; all forms of cooperation, and especially in the villages, were developing in a remarkable way (*Dunlop*, p. 445).

219

[8] *Between Capitalism and Socialism* (New York, 1970), p. 85. Subsequent references to this edition will be included in the text.

[9] In his influential but glib review of *August 1914* in the *New York Review of Books*, Philip Rahv says that "one of the dominant motifs of the novel" is a "technocratic mystique." Rahv categorizes Solzhenitsyn as a "nationalist and a patriot, a belated *narodnik* whose mystic-religious populism oddly accords with his technological and pragmatic inclinations. There is an inherent contradiction, and a rather bizarre one at that, in trying to combine the two positions. . . ." (Rahv's review is reprinted in *Dunlop*, pp. 356–364.) But there is no such contradiction. Rahv's mistake is shared by many critics who feel compelled to "clarify" Solzhenitsyn by labelling him, a way of cutting him down to size.

[10] The latest scholarly book to touch on these matters is Norman Stone, *The Eastern Front, 1914–1917* (New York, 1976). Stone does *not* believe that Tannenberg was the beginning of a series of unmitigated disasters for Russia. As Dorothy Atkinson points out: "From the voluminous literature on Tannenberg two distinct interpretations emerge. Weighed in the larger balance of history Tannenberg is seen as tragic necessity—or as a needless tragedy" (*Dunlop*, p. 425).

[11] Alexander Schmemann believes that the root cause of the Russian failure was not individual men but "a false myth" which paralyzed the country, a myth "stuffed with pseudo-messianism and pseudo-mysticism, and with that spiritual deceit that authentic spirituality so fears" (*Dunlop*, p. 387).

220

SELECTED BIBLIOGRAPHY

Björkegren, Hans. *Aleksandr Solzhenitsyn: A Biography.* New York: The Third Press, 1972.

Burg, David, and George Feifer. *Solzhenitsyn.* New York: Stein & Day, 1972.

Dunlop, John B., Richard Haugh, and Alexis Klimoff, eds. *Aleksandr Solzhenitsyn: Critical Essays and Documentary Records.* Belmont, Mass.: Nordland, 1973.

Fiene, Donald. *Alexander Solzhenitsyn: An International Bibliography of Writings By and About Him, 1962–1973.* Ann Arbor: Ardis, 1973.

Grazzini, Giovanni. *Solzhenitsyn.* London: Michael Joseph, 1973.

Labedz, Leopold, ed. *Solzhenitsyn: A Documentary Record*. Bloomington: Indiana University Press, 1973.

Lukács, George. *Solzhenitsyn*. Cambridge, Mass.: M.I.T. Press, 1971.

Nivat, Georges, and Michel Aucouturier, eds. *Soljénitsyne*. Paris: L'Herne, 1971.

Rothberg, Abraham. *Aleksandr Solzhenitsyn: The Major Novels*. Ithaca: Cornell U. Press, 1971.

————. *The Heirs of Stalin: Dissidence and the Soviet Regime, 1953–1970*. Ithaca: Cornell U. Press, 1972.

Tàtu, Michel. *Power in the Kremlin: From Khrushchev to Kosygin*. New York: The Viking Press, 1970.